SOMETIMES CRUEL

SHORT STORIES

Demetrius Koubourlis PhD

Axios Eclectics

CONTENTS

PROLOGUE

No, I do not hate my parents. There were times in the heat of anger when genuine hatred flared up in my being. Fortunately for me, I'm incapable of holding a grudge. That does not mean the experiences left no trace. They did, and therein lies their constructive potential.

Most of the stories are autobiographical. A few ("The Beating," "The Flag Caper," and "My First Love") involve physical violence; the first two relate to domestic violence. In my effort to be objectively descriptive, I tried to contextualize the incidents. The war played a massive role, as did my parents' upbringing in their culture. Like it or not, we all are products of some culture. We don't get to choose where or when we are born. We don't get to select our parents. We're "accidental." With enlightenment, we may hope our ability to transcend our birth environment becomes enhanced. This is where social education can be a solution.

However, education is not a guarantee. I've come to believe culture leaves an indelible imprint on people's character and behavior. Most people never rid themselves of their cultural stamp, not even partially. Some don't even want to. And some don't even know they ought to want to.

I've always wanted to. My exposure to world literature and natural character predisposition prepared me for that. I was able to transcend what I thought of as my culture's limitations and selectively choose its desirable elements. I strove to do likewise with each different culture I was exposed to. Although I've come to believe in the truism, "you can take a person out of their country, but you can't take their country out of them," I think you can modify it somewhat!

Time was, unless I thought of my glorious ancient forefathers, I felt shame to be regarded as Greek. I sensed a strong desire to be associated with the best, the best country, the best culture, and the best everything.

Experiences along the way taught me how wrong that desire and approach were.

I'm eclectic. This is reflected in the varied material covered in these stories. There are things about my background it's impossible to change. What I can change for good reasons, I strive to. My family's occasional beatings had a profound effect on me. Although I learned the "right lessons" and drew the correct conclusions, ridding myself of undesirable cultural baggage has not been easy. The cultural imprint has deep roots.

If you asked me what I'd like to return to this life as, I might have a surprising answer. Would I change anything? Of course. Wouldn't anyone? I'm now happy with who I am. I know I've been fortunate in many respects. And I choose to be and feel grateful. My parents grew up in a demanding environment. They raised their family as best as possible, partially in a war setting. It's doubtful that I could have done better in their shoes in fundamental ways as a parent. Putting myself in their position is not a wrong way to gain some perspective.

It's so easy to be a couch critic. When I recall some incidents, I'm not sure I'm being entirely fair in my conclusions. Yes, I present my stories as best as I recollect them, but I should never forget the context, and I feel duty-bound to ask the same of the reader.

My father was nearly executed twice during the Greek three-year civil war (1946-1949). One time, I recall my mother waking us kids up in the middle of the night. Communist guerrillas had come to take my father to the no-questions-asked firing squad. Several men had surrounded my father in our kitchen, the oil lamp providing dim lighting. They were accusing him of something specific he couldn't have done. He raised his shirt and pointed at his recent ulcer operation bandage, insisting he was at the hospital then. While this was happening, my mother was herding us, four kids, into the kitchen corridor to provide the ad hominem background.

They left without taking him along. Phew!!! What a major relief!

My father was taken to an impromptu firing squad in another incident. What saved him was luck. Fortunately, the head of the execution squad was a decent acquaintance who vouched for my father as a good man, presenting no problem to the movement. They let him go.

In yet another incident under the Italian occupation, an Italian sergeant and his subaltern came to buy some meat from Father's butcher shop. The sergeant pointed to a piece of meat my father cut the way he'd always done and put it on the scale. The Italian insisted on removing the bone first before weighing it. My father could be hot-headed at times, no matter what. He refused to do it and hung the piece back up, after which the sergeant arrested him and took him to jail. Might makes right, right? It took the intervention of several people to free him, including a Greek translator who remembered the story years later over Souvlakia on one of my visits home.

Despite it all, my father, my family's beater-in-chief, consistently risked life and limb to keep us fed during the various foreign occupations and internecine conflicts. Who am I to criticize him? Instead, I feel more comfortable acknowledging a debt of gratitude and letting bygones be just that.

"My First Memory" is the first rude awakening of my consciousness, which I recall photographically. It occurred when I was two and a half years old and is wholly collaborated by historical records. "My First Toy" will inform and amuse, while "My First Love" will invoke sympathy and understanding.

"Ephemeral Fame" presents a serendipitous encounter in a Chicago Greek restaurant. "A Message From Afar" takes pet relationships to a higher level, while "The Snake Enchanter" surprises and raises questions about the degree of serpentine sentience. "The Two Thai Restaurants" and "A Matter of Inches" narrate stories with auspicious beginnings but tragic ends. While "From the Ministry" will inform and entertain, "Ode to Life" will incite somber thoughts about life and beyond. Its uniqueness will impress as it contains a melody that came to me in a dream, which I captured and recorded in musical notation and presented in a guitar and quasi-polyphonic rendition.

Finally, I couldn't resist the temptation to translate two of my stories, one from English to Spanish and one into English, which I had authored in Greek. A couple of the stories are not autobiographical. I slipped them into this collection as a sample of things to come. See if you can tell which is which. I used Microsoft's AI technology to generate evocative, impressionistic digital art illustrations for the book cover and each story.

Over the years, several people found time to read and comment on some of my writing; I'm thankful to all of them. In the last phase of this compendium, Leslie Sullins, a special friend, proved extremely helpful with proofreading and readying the document for publication – sincere thanks belong to her.

Happy reading!

The Beating

He held both of the little boy's hands high, straight up with his left hand. And with his doubled belt in the other hand, he delivered the cruel strokes.

Whup-thup. Whup-thup!

Mercilessly rhythmical; angrily business-like. Yes, he would teach the little "kerata" (rascal) a good lesson, a lesson never to forget.

Whup-thup. Whup-thup!

The boy's frightful cries pierced the small diner's ambient noise, his little limbs flailing all over as his welted, tender skin reverberated with every whup. The few customers present looked on eagerly as if it were the Roman arena or a welcome sideshow.

Beating one's child is not civilized behavior; I hope you agree. However, contextualizing the whipping of my brother in an environment where civilization had gone awry sheds a somewhat different light on my father's behavior. This was in the early nineteen forties: Second World War lawlessness, desolation, misery, and wretchedness – all man-made - - cruel, idiotic humanity in high gear. Life was iffy; the times were anti-life -- extreme violence reigned supreme. A lot of damage had been done to civilization. People were killed by the thousands, blood flowed all over, and food was scarce. The Italians and the Germans had occupied Greece, and a strict curfew was in place. 60,000 Greek Jews, mainly from Salonica, were herded cattle-like for shipment to forced labor or extermination camps.

I remember witnessing some of the transit as a four-year-old. The railroad station was kitty-corner from our house. It was the point where two tracks had been laid down to facilitate the passage of cross-traveling trains. One train would wait on the side track while the other, going the opposite direction, was allowed to pass.

I recall loitering between the tracks and ogling the people inside the freight wagons more than once. German soldiers would stand, machine guns ready, on either side of each freight car door. The doors on one side would be left open during the stop to let more air in. They and the small windows on either side were barred with barbed wire. Nothing can erase my memory of the faces of exhausted, unkempt people packed like cattle and destined for places like Auschwitz for exploitation and extermination.

I was a little boy -- hardly taller than the German boots I walked by – I was not prevented from looking at the awful spectacle.

This was a most uncivilized environment; I know you'll agree. How does war butchery compare with child beating? Do you suppose violence is contagious?

As a child, my father was orphaned and had been beaten. The culture condoned beating and even recognized it as a primary means of effective discipline.

My father was a resourceful man. He was a successful butcher and a multifaceted businessman. My preschooler brother and I were regularly tasked with shepherding the few goats and sheep our father could wrangle from the mountainous villages on the other side of Rion Strait. These animals were to be butchered at the end of each week.

It was a dangerous trek to defy the curfew by crossing the strait's hazardous winter waters on a small rowboat in the dark of the night. However, my courageous father risked it successfully and repeatedly. Thanks to his efforts, we never went hungry at a time when people were literally dropping dead on the streets from lack of nutrition.

On the fateful day of the beating, one of the goats slipped away from the rest and simply walked into the sea before we could turn it around. We were small and frightened, powerless and on our own. We called it back, and we yelled and cried. We waved our sticks in desperation and threw pebbles in its path to turn it around, to no avail. The stubborn goat paddled on ploddingly deeper and deeper as if possessed by a death wish or a yearning to find its home or mate across the strait. And our fearful little children's hearts sank lower and lower. My entire pre-school self was filled with fear: fear of the whirling waters – we were at the point of the cape, where one of the townsfolk had recently drowned -- and fear of our father: how could we explain the loss of his goat?

My brother was about a year and a half my senior. As he was getting viciously belted, I ran my fastest to get our mother from the backroom to plead with my father to stop the beating. She and I rushed to the restaurant's corner, where the wicked performance occurred. But my mother stopped short of physically intervening. She only whimpered:

"Come on, John. Let him go," (Μικρό παιδί' ναι,) "he's just a little kid."

Disappointed by my mother's faint-hearted helplessness and without wasting any precious moments, I whooshed between my brother and father, my nose bumping onto his knee. I pounded on my father's thighs, tears streaming down my face. I screamed and cried:

"You're killing him! Let him go now! Let him gooooo!" But he pushed me forcefully aside, intent to continue.

However, the boldness of a five-year-old had an instant profound effect on the scene. From a socially approved disciplinary action, the beating suddenly morphed into an act of cruelty. My swiftly emboldened mother grabbed hold of the belting arm as if possessed. My father took notice. A furtive glance at the few diners around -- their now disapproving faces produced a sudden change in him. And as if by a puncture, his anger deflated as quickly as it had exploded. His hold on my brother went loose. He mumbled some of his usual insults while putting his belt back on.

I felt immensely relieved. I had rescued my brother and possibly myself, as my turn would have likely been next. This was not the first beating, nor would it be the last during our years with Father. The only choice for us children and my mother was submission. The patriarchal order was strict -- we couldn't even conceive of raising a hand against the father. Doing so would have indicated disrespect, an improperly functioning family, and one in which established tradition had not taken root. I took my brother by the hand to the back room, our bedroom. He curled up on our shared bed, still howling like a wounded dog, and I sat beside him, patting his forehead and comforting him. And it felt right; I had initiated and gotten the rescue done and made a small dent in a vast cultural defect.

There is a streak of a freedom fighter or an independence advocate in me. I would occasionally irritate and anger my father with my penchant for fearlessly pointing out contradictions. Time and again, I remember being told that I had no right to "have nerves" as a child. I understood that my child's rights were non-existent and only what my parents would ad-hoc grant me.

My father was not happy with me for yet another reason. I would not help him kill an animal for our butcher shop. No amount of coaxing could get me to do that. However, my brother did. Needless to say, I was not then his favorite son, and neither was I my mother's.

My father could run very fast. And so could I. I must have inherited that trait from him, which may be why I'm still alive. I vividly remember my father with a knife in his right-hand close at my heels, sprinting at full speed, but I don't recall why. It was one early summer afternoon, which must have been during my early teenage years. Full of mortal fear, I could feel him furiously running close behind me. He was as angry as can be and eager to use the knife, but I thankfully managed to outrun him. I stayed away from the house, wandering chilled and hungry in the vineyard nearby for many hours. No family member dared defy my father by coming to my assistance. I had to wait long hours for my father to turn in for the night before I could return, grab something to eat, and go to sleep.

Would you say knives are a butcher's weapon of choice? Do you think it's easier for a butcher to kill with a knife or to kill at all? For the record, my father never killed anyone. Well, almost.

I had nearly forgotten another incident until my brother reminded me a few years ago. My father provided very well for us, but sometimes, some things were extremely scarce. This is most likely one of the times when the following incident occurred.

Our father was enjoying an orange after our family lunch while the rest of us, four children and my mother, looked on – no oranges for us. Being the way I am, I couldn't resist pointing that out. Not wasting a microsecond, my father grabbed the sharp knife he'd been using to peel the orange and threw it at me like a dart. Anticipating his aim, I lightning-like sidestepped out of the way at the last instant. However, the knife settled in the right forearm of my poor mother, who happened to be standing behind me. Thankfully, she recovered and even received a small disability pension in addition. I still cringe at this outcome as I sense a lack of reckoning and dishonesty. I see my father getting away with what I considered opprobrious behavior time and again, and I can't condone his conniving complicity in securing the disability benefit.

Sooner or later, everything ends, from major events like wars to minor ones like beatings.

Once, my father cornered me in our back storage room, where our giant, horizontally-arrayed wine barrels rested. I must have been about fourteen at the time. He started hitting me with abandon, his belt rising and falling rapidly. As ill luck would have it, I stumbled and fell while backing up against the barrels to avoid the strokes. I was lying on my back; his body was blocking the exit; I was trapped. There was no way out! Realizing his advantage, he eagerly bent over me to continue his dirty deed. I quickly brought my legs as close as I could to my chest, and with all the might both of my legs could simultaneously muster, I kicked him in the groin. It had to have been my most powerful kick, born of absolute desperation and indignation, and it had to have hurt a lot. I floored him. I quickly got up and scrambled from the scene.

He never laid his hands on me ever again.

Boquete, Panama
January 2022.

A Matter of Inches

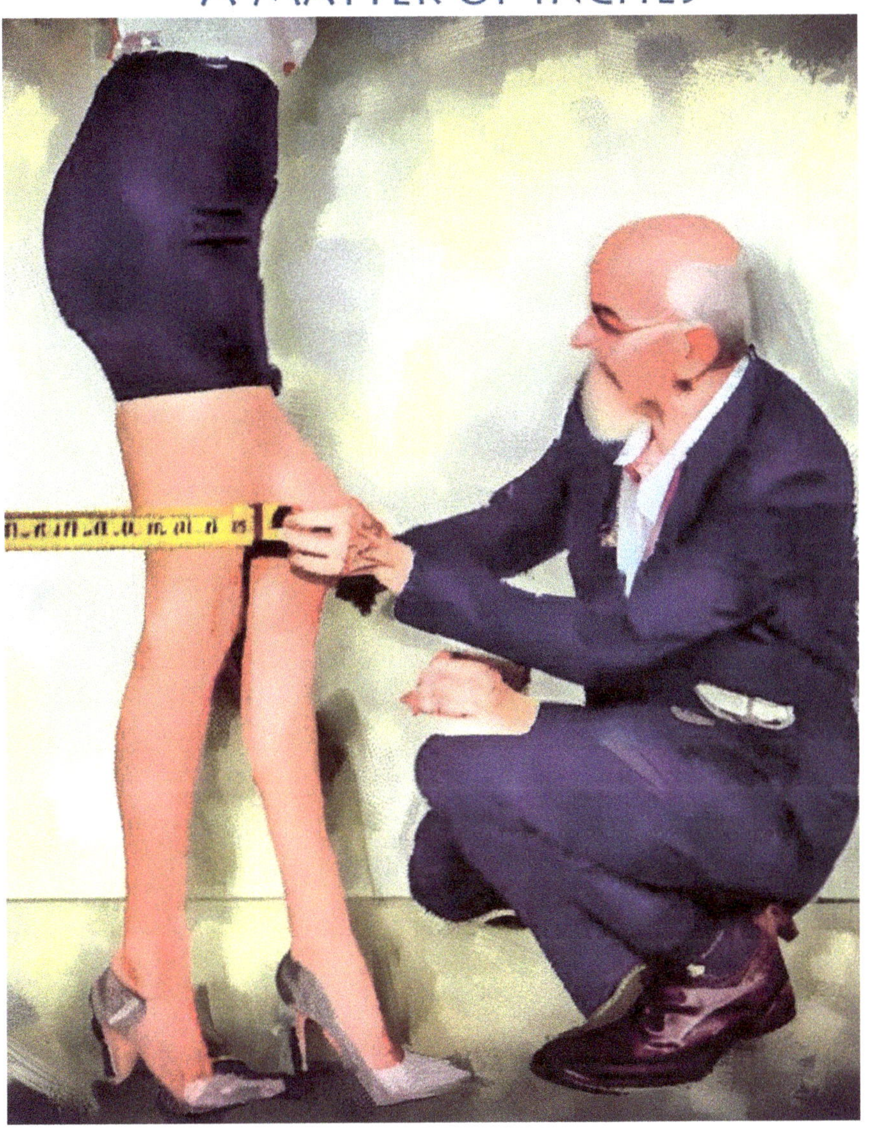

S uppose you were to stroll westward in Vancouver, BC, past China Town, then toward Stanley Park, and just before you enter the West End proper –- that's where you'd find a score of tailor shops. They offer all kinds of alterations and custom tailoring. It would not surprise you to chance upon tailors from various countries. Among them, you'd find immigrants or refugees evading hunger or persecution, hoping to make and send money back home to needy relatives, or simply seeking a better life for themselves and their future families.

A plant, you'll agree, does not leave the native soil voluntarily and usually thrives where its roots take hold. People, too, would rather stay swathed by the protective cocoon of their culture, surrounded by what they know and feel comfortable with. But not always. Some plants flourish in a new environment, and so do some people when the relocation conditions are favorable, or the native soil is barren.

If you were to set your calendar approximately sixty years back and ask around in Vancouver about the best custom tailor, you would not fail to notice Pepe's name mentioned more than once. (The nickname "Pepe" is short for Italian Giuseppe.)

Pepe was born and raised in a mountainous Italian village. He had gotten an elementary school education like most people in his community. The nearest high school was far away, and public transportation was lacking. Like most people in his village, his family was poor, and primary education had sufficed for countless generations.

How can a poorly-educated immigrant with zero language skills and no funds succeed? Through contacts or luck, would you say? How far can those take one? Millions leave their birthplace, and most manage to make a decent life for themselves. Immigrants are well-known for their ambitiousness, work ethic, resourcefulness, and flexibility. While their "hunger" powers whatever success they achieve, true talent can supercharge their success. Talent is a scarce gift of nature, difficult to hide or inhibit; it's like an unstoppable elemental force. However, even the most rarefied of talents can be thwarted absent favorable conditions; nothing new here.

Soon after Pepe arrived in Vancouver, he landed a job thanks to a distant relative. As he didn't know English, the best he could do was to work as a dishwasher in one of the many Italian restaurants. Soon, he was promoted to busboy and could observe the clientele and rejoice in the merry sounds of his native tongue, as many of the clients were Italian.

Pepe's keen eye turned to studying well-dressed people. His glance acted like a measuring stick. He instinctively took in proportions and readily "felt" what looked good and didn't. Gathering dirty dishes day in and day out can be tedious, but not when your mind brings creativity to the table. Pepe's mind crystallized specific proportions as good and disregarded or even disdained what he considered the wrong kind. Gradually, he was becoming some kind of an elitist — an uneducated, self-taught elitist.

Pepe started paying more attention to his own clothing as well. He had been wearing his best clothes on the job; this was what his poor family back home was able to provide for him. But soon, he felt "ashamed" of the style and the lines. His sense told him his attire was *peasant-like*. Not the right kind. A powerful inner force urged him to act. With his first paycheck, he bought a terrific-looking pair of pants and an elegant shirt. His co-workers couldn't fail to notice the change. Pepe's journey of separation from the crowd had begun. He even started walking somewhat differently; he held his chin higher, and his facial expressions assumed an "aristocratic air." Something new was being born. Pepe looked and moved about as if possessed by some mysterious force.

His co-workers, however, weren't particularly pleased. Who was *he* to act with that sort of aplomb in their midst? Who was this villager dishwasher/busboy to behave like that? In short, Pepe's demeanor, displayed with pomp, made him unpopular, and the general grumbling came to a head. One day, when Pepe came to work, his somber-faced boss asked him to step into the office. Without any explanation, he was told his services were no longer needed. He was handed his final paycheck and summarily dismissed.

Pepe was shaken at his core. Try as he might, he could not grasp what had gone wrong. He had never missed a day and was always on time. Moreover, he collected the dishes faster than anyone else and hadn't even broken a single plate the entire time. Deeply distraught and jobless, Pepe walked the streets in a mental haze. Soon, he found himself somewhere in the "tailor district."

"POSTI DI LAVORO DISPONIBILI" (Jobs available) read a sign in Italian on a large window beside a male mannequin. With his mind still befogged by his dismissal earlier that day, he lingered before the display a while longer before walking further. Suddenly, as if a giant hand had clutched him, he turned around and retraced his steps. He entered the store as if in a trance. The employees' first thought was that Pepe was a prospective customer -- his allure and attire certainly exuded that impression.

"Si parla italiano qui?" (Is Italian spoken here?) he asked.

"Of course, we're all Italians here," he was informed in all readiness to be of service.

"Dov'è il capo?" (Where's the boss?) he asked impatiently.

He was offered a job as an apprentice with minimal pay. Without losing any time, Pepe set out to distinguish himself. He executed all assigned tasks with distinction and soon extended his touch to innovative suggestions, pleasing customers who took notice. His differentness was quickly spotted. More and more technically demanding tasks were given to him. He outperformed all expectations. Soon, he was measuring customers and actively participating in sewing expensive men's suits! Several regular patrons, many quite wealthy, would ask for him and him alone, or else.

Pepe had found his element. If life has a reservoir of gems at its disposal, which it sprinkles sparingly here and there, Pepe's talent would have been one of them. He was gratified and successful and acquired his own shop a few years later. His customers never left him; they brought him their friends, who in turn brought their own friends, and so on. Pepe's business mushroomed. He was able to hire other tailors and grow even faster. In only a dozen years, his shop came to be ranked among the best in the area. His list of clients included some of the wealthiest Vancouverites and even some well-known politicians.

Pepe was more in the mold of a clothes designer without an innovative flourish; he could improve any existing design. His fine-tuning modifications would accentuate the beautiful and de-emphasize the ugly. Slight changes in suits would make the wearer look more robust and augment sex appeal. He was a master of interpreting any design to exceed the designer's vision and the client's expectations. This is where his divine talent lay. Even the untrained eye could perceive there was something super-special in his work. His customers, if asked, would not be able to describe it but would all agree they liked it. Pepe's work engendered a "wow" feeling that rippled especially in the hearts of the frivolous.

His extraordinariness would not have revealed itself if he had stayed in his native mountain village. No way. The demand for his inordinate talent would have never exceeded the ordinary. His transplantation to Vancouver provided the impetus for glorious growth. What made this possible was the rapidly growing demand. In a big cosmopolitan city, tastes get refined and quickly establish themselves as the new norm in sophisticated competition. Enclaves of high society get established. Ways to delineate themselves develop — people want to look their best, and many confuse actual personal worthiness with the current fashion. Fashion, Couture, and Haute Couture provide an easy and obvious way to convert money into individual value. Perhaps the less valuable a person's interior worth, the more necessary a dazzling exterior disguise. Vanity fuels the process -- to look better, feel better, impress others, and somehow distinguish oneself. The fashion industry knows and exploits this.

This was the new soil where Pepe was resettled. And he thrived.

However, with this undeniable success, certain undesirable personality traits began manifesting themselves. Pepe's growing elitist attitude turned to sheer snobbism; he looked down upon everything that wasn't to his liking. He would mistreat his employees and would occasionally explode indignantly in macaronic Italian-English at what he considered inexcusable mistakes. In short, he displayed a tyrannical side of his personality that pleased no one. Some employees could not take it and left. No one dared cut him down to size. Yet, the quality of his product remained superior.

Fast forward to many years later.

Pepe's Tailor Shop in Vancouver had been in business for a long time. It was an excellent place to get a first-class suit for a fair price. As he grew older, Pepe delegated more and more of the work to others but always made himself available to greet customers and even take their orders. His autocratic treatment of his employees was contrasted against a distinctively obsequious behavior toward his customers.

And the business continued to expand beyond anyone's wildest expectations.

How often does a tailor shop get a seven-million-dollar contract to sew uniforms? Once in a lifetime, maybe, provided Lady Luck chooses to smile. At Canadian Air, the corporate management voted on a change in flight attendant attire. They hired a well-known designer and tasked him to submit drawings. After carefully choosing the final design, Pepe's Tailor Shop was awarded the contract. Pepe was elated. So was everyone working at his shop and all his suppliers upon hearing the good news; only his competitors were filled with envy.

It became necessary to hire additional people. Old Pepe decided he should postpone that long-planned trip to his native Italy. Now was not the time to go visiting relatives and relatives' graves. Now came the moment to make some good money. It had taken a long time to land this contract. For more than twenty-five years in the tailoring business, he wouldn't even dare dream of a single transaction this big. Yes, there was no doubt in his mind that Italy and all the relatives, dead or alive, could wait. There is a season to go visiting and a season to make money. Which season was now, Pepe knew beyond the slightest doubt.

Delegating tasks had become Pepe's chief hobby in the last decade of his business. Pepe had long realized that there is only so much money a tailor, even the best tailor, can make by the sweat of his brow. Expanding was needed — more master tailor employees, customers, and suits. A grade school education in his native mountain village had not prepared him for big business. Yet, endowed with more common sense than most mortals, he learned by observing, asking questions, experimenting, and occasionally reading. Over the years, Pepe had amassed a good repertory of facts and notions on business growth. His discernment, guided by his innate talent, resulted in a well-functioning personal business philosophy. And one might agree that Pepe had successfully implemented some of his painstakingly acquired knowledge. In recent years, Pepe, still in good health but somewhat advancing in age, had worked less and less. Some days, he wouldn't even make it to work. Was he becoming a victim of his own success? With time, even the most exciting occupation falls victim to tedium.

But the big airline contract changed all that. Pepe correctly reasoned that he had to put his shoulder to the wheel until this godsend of a contract was fulfilled.

Tailors often get in trouble because someone less attentive in the shop takes the wrong measurements. Correct measuring is the first and possibly the most important of all the tasks associated with suit-making. So, it was no surprise that he reserved the measuring job for himself. Traditionally, tailors fit men's clothing mostly. With increasing frequency, however, unisexual dress codes ushered in a noticeable change in clientele. Pepe's had somehow managed to remain a man's shop. It had always been a shop for men and continued until the big airline contract came along.

On any day and as the flight schedule would permit, whole crews would drop in to get measured. For every male flight attendant, there came a slew of stewardesses. In came blondes and brunettes, short and tall, young and not so young, skinny and not so skinny. More than anyone else, Pepe had much adjusting to do. For years, fitting men was a simple routine -- you measure here and there. The job takes minutes.

Yet, measuring female flight attendants for pants presented a particular problem in determining the in-seam without touching the mons pubis and without appearing indiscreet and embarrassing. The problem wasn't as bad if the ladies wore pants when they came in. When they wore skirts or dresses, however, it was like walking a land mine. Poor old Pepe was at a loss. He tried his professional best, thought of polite ways to broach the question, and even asked the girls to take that crucial measurement themselves. Still, he couldn't always be sure they had measured correctly. To the uninitiated, measuring to fit may seem like a simple job. Well, it is simple only if you know what you are doing.

Soon, the self-measuring yielded a crop of dissatisfied customers and resulted in second and third trials. Pepe's long experience clearly told him this was bad for business. Poor workmanship and ill-fitting uniforms meant not only complaining customers and subsequent loss of potential business but also loss of precious time. Finally, the situation got out of hand. It had become so bad that Pepe had difficulty sleeping. Tossing and turning one night, he decided he had had enough of mismeasurements and would do the sizing himself, just like he had done for many years. Male or female, legs are legs, he reasoned: measurements must be determined the first time correctly if pants should fit, tough if someone didn't like it.

So, with the purest professional intentions, Pepe approached his measuring work the following morning. Resolutely, he proceeded to take the measurements of his first female customer.

Having lost sleep, Pepe was unusually nervous. Habit took over, and, in his thick Italian accent, he fired off the first question that he would pose to any and all of his male customers while measuring for pants:

"Do you hang your Pistola on the right or the left?" The young flight attendant didn't quite understand.

"Pistol?" she asked, her innocent mind searching and fortunately never guessing the maladroit reference to the male anatomy.

Poor Pepe felt more embarrassed than ever and sought a quick way to move on with it. Still fearing the worst, he saved the crotch measurement for last. Taking a deep breath and looking aside as if discreetly, he raised the measuring tape up to you-know-where, one hand holding one end of the tape at the bottom and the other holding the other end at the top. Still, his trembling didn't help matters. Having touched the sensitive area more resolutely than necessary, poor professional Pepe recoiled in fear.

Or was it some kind of excitement?

He couldn't say. And most probably, *he would not say*. But it must have gone relatively well, judging by the lack of unusual reaction on the stewardess' face.

With time, even old dogs learn new tricks. Pepe became more and more proficient at securing this critical measurement. He would even accompany the act with pleasant conversation, seemingly unrelated to the task. Tumbling inhibitions, however, know not when to stop. When motivated by man's most substantial drive, boldness takes the upper hand rather rapidly. Pepe began enjoying the crotch measurement -- tailoring had never been this much fun. He was making a pile of money and having the time of his life simultaneously. There was a time when he would have paid good money for the privilege.

Libidinous audacity quickly blinds even the wisest of men; it turns wise men into fools; it changes sheep to wolves and bears to bulls. Pepe naughtily introduced a flipping maneuver –- while taking the in-seam measurement, he'd quickly cup his palm and flip it upward to increase the contact with the coveted area. Whether it was lasciviousness or lechery caused by advancing age was not apparent. But what became exceedingly clear was the clamor of rumors and, finally, complaints that began their age-old course.

One day, Lady Luck frowned upon Pepe's Tailor Shop just as suddenly as it had smiled. Canadian Air's complaints file had grown very thick, and the company suddenly decided to take immediate action in the best tradition of managerial efficacy. To Pepe's greatest chagrin, the 7-million-dollar contract got unceremoniously canceled. Reason given:

"Unprofessional conduct. Early termination compensation clause #15 does not apply."

Pepe needed no further explanation. He realized he'd gotten in deep trouble but felt too ashamed to discuss it with anyone. He knew he'd been taking risks with his liberties, but his waning libido had pushed him into supernova mode. The abrupt cancelation hit him hard. He wilted like a freshly cut flower thrown in hot water. Pepe, in his heart, had remained a primitive villager. His sartorial sophistication was in complete contrast with all else. His brief marriage brought him only problems he could not understand, much less solve. And he ended up living alone.

I met Pepe soon afterward on Maui. He and I were staying in a shared condo. A permanently locked door separated a two-bedroom condo into two independent units at Nani Kai Hale, a popular beach complex. My rusty Italian (after two decades of inactivity) quickly became the glue that held the responsive camaraderie together. We took a few walks together in the early morning; he would wade at the water's edge as I took my morning swim in Maalaea Bay. Maui had become a very popular winter sojourn for Canadian "snowbirds." Unlike most sun-seekers, Pepe, profoundly distraught after losing the airline contract, had come to Maui to heal a festering wound.

Poor Pepe opened his heart to me; he revealed I was the first person he managed to share his pain with. I could feel his suffering; he could not talk about anything else. It was the shame, not the failed contract, that was consuming him. He had lost face, and his pride was devastated. He was a vessel adrift and listing.

"Beh, tutto è perduto, tutto è perduto" (Well, all is lost, all is lost), he would say as if in mantra mode. In vain, did I try my best to take his mind off that subject. But the thought tormented him. More than once, I became the unintentional witness to his profound pain — through the shared door, I would hear him sob and even wail at night. I could easily empathize, and I felt genuinely sorry for him. Then, one night, I overheard what must have been a loud bawl consisting of a single protracted vowel, which seemed to be issuing from his innermost innards. His unbearable pain was climaxing, exploding. Such *involuntary* sounds are sometimes called the "primal scream." They have been known to mark an actual evolution in handling deep-rooted psychological pain.

I set out for my morning walk on Kihei Beach the following morning. To my surprise, Pepe was sitting on one of the condominium lawn chaises, having an animated conversation with another Italian vacationer. They talked about the Old Country and cracked jokes. The minute he saw me approaching, Pepe got up to shake my hand; he asked how I was doing, showing genuine interest. I'd never seen Pepe so lively in the several days since we'd met. Gone was the sadness from his face; his torso looked straightened out and more vibrant than I'd seen during any of the preceding days.

Looking at his altered state, I couldn't contain my joy. He invited me on the long drive around the island and suggested we have lunch at Hana, the island's north side – he was buying, he emphasized. I rejoiced in the transformation and drew the only conclusion possible – Pepe was turning or already had turned the corner. He was going to be alright.

Or was he?

Pepe was like a square boulder able to roll despite shape and gravity. He had always dealt with his problems and managed them somehow. There was a good chance he'd pull through this time, too.

Pepe was a proud man. His masculine pride would provide the wherewithal to surmount obstacles. I've often wondered if pride is a necessary ingredient for success or can also be the cause of failure. Whether or not he was aware, Pepe's sense of self-worth must have been higher than average. His lack of education couldn't assist him in his internal inferno — can education help anyway? Turning to a "shrink" was out of the question. Poor Pepe was alone, as pride prevented him from accepting conciliatory input.

Indeed, great talent can bring success and joy, but not only.

At the end of his two-week stay, he knocked on my door; he was catching a morning flight back home. He wrapped his arms around me and held me tight for an inordinately long time. Then he kissed my cheeks, right-left-right, not according to the occasional European custom, but as if performing a solemn act. Next, he gently pushed me back, locking his eyes on mine while a nascent tear slowly rolled down his cheek.

"See you next year, right here," I said wishfully. Pepe closed his eyes momentarily and nodded with what I perceived as a forced smile. I walked with him to his rented car in the parking lot below. We hugged one more time. He got into his car and waved goodbye.

Three weeks later, I got a terse message from a mutual friend: Pepe was no more.

Pullman, Washington,
August 2022

People want to have fun. They find ways to smile, laugh, sing, and dance even in the dreariest places. A Belarusian holiday of great mirth, known as Kupalski Vyanok, comes around July 8. If traveling in these parts during this holiday, one is well-advised to keep that in mind. Late one afternoon, my Belarusian companion and I promptly got lost after driving to Mogilev, a good-sized provincial town of about three hundred and fifty thousand peaceful inhabitants with a rich inter-ethnic history.

Belarusians are descendants of the East Slav tribes and linguistically belong to the East Slavic group (Russians, Ukrainians, and Belarusians). Poles, Lithuanians, Jews, and gypsies have contributed to the cultural blend. When not invaded, the people here have occasionally concocted ways to battle amongst themselves while harmoniously co-existing most of the time.

As is well known, people do not like wars; instead, they prefer to get along, trade and have fun, live and let live until some megalomaniac comes along to stir up their souls. Noxious notions like religious fanaticism, nationalism, and even jingoism can poison the minds of otherwise tranquil humans. Super-aggressive pursuits of equality can divide the populace -- the haves and have-nots, you know -- and off they go, mindlessly killing and getting killed. Havoc. Mayhem. Chaos.

When we arrived at our destination, about forty minutes late, our reserved apartment had been given to someone else. No amount of civilized reasoning could change that unpleasant fact. With access to the internet, however, we placed numerous calls searching for a replacement, but without success. We begged, pleaded, and offered to pay just about any price – to no avail. Evidently, a lot of holiday traveling -- a significant temporary and voluntary population displacement -- was afoot. People anywhere and everywhere need holiday time.

We then started calling out-of-town places and even canvased Shklov -- Lukashenko's birthplace -- without success. Next, we increased the radius further, one hundred plus kilometers. An obliging landlady informed us that all her places were taken up, but a friend might have something; she promised to check and call us back. While waiting for her reply, we made a few additional calls without luck.

With all hope lost and actually sobbing in utter desperation – can you believe it? -- Tanya, my Belarusian companion, knelt on the ground, crossing herself in the Greek-Russian Orthodox manner and praying for divine assistance. I gazed at this odd spectacle on officially atheist soil in dazed disbelief as my cultural horizon was getting strained.

Within minutes, however, by coincidence or divine intervention, it happened. The ground did not shake, and the heavens did not get torn asunder, but the caring landlady called back. She gave us the phone number of a friend whose father might be willing to let us stay in a room in his dacha, his summer home. There was no indoor plumbing or openable windows, and the cost would be $40 for two nights! We agreed to take it immediately without further discussion or the slightest hesitation. (Tanya is still convinced that, thanks to her fervent prayers, we had a place to stay for the next two nights and that it was only a few kilometers away from our next 12-day stop! Try as I might, I was unsuccessful in persuading her that God does not help with reservations.)

The roads in Belarus are fun to drive: straight and ample with few cars, clean and functional with endless birch forests stretching heavenward, elegantly gracing the landscape everywhere. I like the Belarusian countryside.

And I love Belarusians. They're hospitable and eager to share their last morsel with you. More than once, I was made to feel welcome and at home. My being, at the core, unpretentious and able to communicate with them in their language hasn't hurt either. I've found myself accepted in their midst within minutes of presenting myself, joking and laughing with goodwill flowing all around. I've been made to feel, I dare say, like one of them more than once. Thank you, Belarus!

Three hours later, we arrived at our place of last resort. It was a typical Belarusian country house, a dacha, built a couple of generations ago and adorned with a light blue, yellow, and green accent; multi-colored variations abound here. On its wall facing the alley, a shiny bronze plaque prominently projected the owner's name and his post: Ivan Victorovich Maroz, Chief of the Village.

In the chief's absence, his son-in-law and two daughters, accompanied by a small girl, welcomed us warmly and offered us whatever extras we required for comfort. I gave the little girl a couple of dollars, and all went even better. They led us across the road, down a short path overgrown with lush greenery, past a large country bathhouse, and down some discarded truck tire steps. As we rounded the voluminous bushes, a small lake came into view; we were told we could swim there in complete privacy.

Good people.

Thus, we got gratefully settled into our sight-unseen last available room in this part of Belarus on that festive weekend of Kupalski Vyanok. It featured no indoor bathroom or openable windows but offered other amenities.

Early the following day, a colossal man, whom I presumed to be the owner, appeared; he entered the kitchen area adjoining and facing our room. As the only supply of air, our door was open, and I was seated in my full lotus position. We glanced at each other, and I introduced myself but got no response. I didn't know what to think other than that he might be deaf, that I might be speaking a language he didn't understand, or that my odd yoga asana might have puzzled him speechless.

A powerfully shouldered mountain of a man, Ivan Victorovich, literally filled the kitchen. Compared to some policemen elsewhere, one could not confuse his bulk for fat. His commanding appearance was augmented by his blue uniform cum stars and echelons and his umbrella of a police hat, typical of Soviet and post-Soviet times, designed to intimidate. As it turned out, Ivan Victorovich Maroz -- the village Chief and our host -- was also the head of the nearest town's police department.

No, he didn't arrest me. And he even proved capable of occasional voice articulation.

If our host's appearance created a menacing impression, the man himself was anything but frightening. He proved to be among the most obliging people I've ever known. As I had planned to have some dental work done in Belarus, Tanya thought it a good idea to inquire if our host would recommend a dentist in his town. He was eager to help. He said there would be no problem and invited us to meet him at his office the following day.

Belarus – and this is a little-known fact -- is a country where excellent and inexpensive medical care abounds. Many expatriates return to their homeland, killing two birds with one stone – visiting their land and accessing high-quality medical care at a meager cost.

The next day we went to the "big" town. We had no difficulty locating the Police Station. "Just ask anyone; it's near Lenin Square," the Chief had said. The first person we asked pointed in the desired direction while at the same time quizzically looking at us as if wondering why anyone would want to go there. It was in a fortress of a building. The Chief had left instructions to let us in. We had to announce ourselves through an intercom before the heavy metal door could open. We were ushered into a grandiose office festooned with all the trappings of power. Ivan Victorovich was wrapped around his massive desk -- a good match of proportions, I thought.

After a few silent moments, punctuated by meaningful glances allowing us to digest the awesomeness of his position, he got up and led us out of his office. He got into his car and asked us to follow him. We were headed to the dentistry polyclinic (Стоматологическая Поликлиника), a large building devoted entirely to dentistry. The Chief quickly found out which office to go to.

We hurriedly climbed to the second floor, where more than two dozen people were waiting in the unlit corridor to see precisely the specialist we needed. No matter; the Chief casually marched to the head of the line and opened the dentist's door without knocking. After a few seconds, he came out instructing me to enter together with the next person – he pointed to an overweight lady at the head of the very long line! With Tanya close behind and my sense of justice and propriety conveniently dormant, I sheepishly followed the voluminous lady into the dentist's work area. There was a loud cacophony in protest from the long line, which we conveniently ignored, closing the door behind us.

We were invited to sit down, and after less than a minute, I was placed in the dentist's chair! I explained to the dentist what I wanted to be done. She looked at my teeth carefully and said it would involve replacing two crowns, which had to be worked on simultaneously. However, she could not do it herself because she was going on vacation. Still, she recommended a private practitioner who could do it well and quickly. I was relieved that it wouldn't be this ancient lady doctor. The suspicion was that the old lady may have outdated technology.

When we got out, the scrawny lady at the head of the line resumed her attack about our having cut in line. I wasted no time telling her that she needn't have worried as it had only taken a minute. But sanctified and buoyed by the ambient chorus, she continued undeterred with her litany of protestations. Evidently, her sense of propriety was similar, if not identical, to mine, and I instinctively knew how to shut her up. Looking at her straight in the eyes, I stepped closer and said, "You're right" (вы правы) before proceeding to exit. This shut her and the others up instantly. They had expected a counter-argument, as is the norm here; instead, they got an immediate civilized admission – they were floored!

Belarusians are easy to like and eager to please. Living in the provinces seems to be more straightforward. One can always find a centrally located farmer's market (рынок) and a mini-market (магазин) in every town and village. Life is tranquil as there are no criminal organizations -- a huge plus.

His considerable aplomb notwithstanding, our trusty Ivan Victorovich was inconspicuously leaning against the wall in the cavernous corridor, waiting for us to come out. We told him the dentist's verdict, and he unhesitatingly elected to lead us to the private clinic the doctor recommended.

There are men of action and men of words. The Chief is definitely a man of action and very few words. He's a man sure of his place in the world; he leaves talking to others -- I found myself filling both sides of our conversation more than once. Regular conversations have a rhythm. There are dialogs and monologs. What I had with the Chief was none of the above. If my primary way is through language, his was through body size and displacement. He was an earthquake of a man, alright. Yet, I was beginning to take a genuine liking to him.

A boiling question began forming in my mind: what had the Chief said or done to get such super-priority treatment for me? Did he threaten? Did he cajole? I didn't like asking him, so I appealed to Tanya. She didn't have a clue either but promised to find out.

Once again, we got into our car and followed him. He drove like a cannon shot – was he trying to impress us, or was this his usual way? I exceeded my personal speed limit, keeping up with him, figuring that this was one time I could break the law without consequences. The experience was intoxicating. I couldn't stop laughing really loud while speeding within city limits. I enjoyed every bit of Ivan Victorovich's VIP treatment; it was a veritable high. Perhaps for a minute, I knew how it feels to be a cop behind the wheel or one of the privileged few -- quite realistic, a vicarious experience. Exhilarating! If there was a racer suppressed in me, escape must have occurred this one time.

After we came to a stop, he led us into the corridor of a dark Soviet-era building, looking at every door in search of the recommended private orthodontist. There was not a soul to be seen. Although clean, it was like a ghost building -- a couple of bicycles were stashed under the stairway. He quickly led us out of there; I had to jog to keep up with his gigantic stride.

Not far from there, we found the doctor's office in a most unattractive building, which seemed to have been abandoned except for this dentist's two rooms in the backside. The Chief barged in ahead of the lady who was next in line without as much as excusing himself. This was the same procedure as before, except that only one person was in line here. The second part of the procedure was quickly repeated. I was signaled to enter, the patient in the dentist's chair was kicked off, and I was enthroned promptly in her place. I was immune to guilt by now. I was getting spoiled and, I must confess, I liked it!

Absolutely no waiting! Can you believe it? This was a great taste of a VIP treatment I will not soon forget. How did our intrepid Ivan Victorovich really do it? What were the magic words he used, if any? What could open doors so quickly or power them open unceremoniously? In search of the mystery of the Chief's magic, Tanya somehow managed to get her head into the door just as our host completed his brief but effective performance. My hopes were raised that we would soon have the answer to the Chief's extraordinary 100% line-cutting success. As soon as I was able to, I excitedly asked Tanya to share her discovery with me, but I was deeply disappointed. She had not captured anything but promised to try next time, should there be any.

The fact that only one person was in this waiting line requires an explanation. Unlike the public dental clinic, where we made our first stop, this was a private clinic where one must pay a lot more for services; hence, the greater the cost, the shorter the line. A list of dental services and their respective prices were prominently displayed in the dentist's waiting room. For example, a crown would cost 55 bucks, a far more significant sum than the few dollars at the public clinic! (Compare that with about a thousand dollars in the States.)

The dentist asked me what I wanted to have done. He listened attentively to my well-rehearsed two-sentence spiel. He looked carefully at the affected teeth and the rest of my dental armature. He then made his pronouncement: he could do it. The next step would be to take X-rays. Without wasting time, he picked up a piece of paper – the eighth of a cut-up page – and scribbled in code indicating which teeth needed to be x-rayed. With that datum in hand, we rushed back to the same dental clinic where we had come from.

This time, though, Ivan Victorovich led us to a different door. He charged in as usual, but as if chained to him, Tanya slipped in right behind him; they both came back out after a few seconds. Tanya was beaming. I surmised something significant had occurred and couldn't wait to get the loot. I was told to stay in the corridor. I was hoping to debrief Tanya right away, but she ran off to the cashier's window (касса) to pay for the X-rays. About a minute later, the door opened, and a person who turned out to be the radiologist asked me to enter. He then pointed to a single chair in the next room. He sat me down, put an X-ray protective apron on me, and, getting ready to take the first X-ray, placed a small film behind one of the target teeth. He then exited the room and, while looking through a special opening in the thick wall, he clicked the beam. The procedure was repeated with the second tooth while I held the film with my left hand. Next, I was ushered back into the corridor and asked to take a seat.

Tanya returned from the cashier, prominently holding a small receipt like a war trophy. As usual, I was curious how much this no-nonsense X-ray operation cost. Before I could even ask, Tanya showed me the receipt, and I gasped! Forty whole CENTS each x-ray!!! My first thought was that there was some kind of an error; my second thought was that I was making a mistake in my rubles-to-dollars conversion. So, I asked Tanya, who happens to be a math whizz, among many things, to verify. No, there was no mistake, she responded, not showing much surprise -- eighty gargantuan cents for both x-rays!

Next, I was anxious to find out what had caused Tanya's earlier radiant look when she exited the radiologist's office. As I posed the question, the radiologist came out with two double-stamp-sized X-rays, still wet. After handing the radiologist the receipt, she dexterously placed one X-ray between the thumb and index and the other between the ring finger and the pinky of her left hand. She carefully kept them apart to dry while returning to the private orthodontist.

Tanya, evidently not wanting to walk with the X-rays half a block away to where my car was, hopped into the Chief's car, which was parked right at the very entry.

It felt as if Tanya was tormenting me by intentionally keeping her findings away from me for a while longer. Did she mean to annoy me? With my curiosity under tantalized control, I followed them, speeding back to the second orthodontist who had ordered the X-rays. The Chief charged ahead of the people waiting in line while Tanya trailed close behind, holding the X-rays head-high as if to show we were in the process. I slipped in after them.

The doctor immediately dropped what he was doing on the patient seated in the chair. He took the X-rays and looked at them against the light. Then he talked about how long it would take, and Tanya informed him about our stay in the area – 12 days. There was plenty of time, he said. He then did some more thinking and said that as the teeth were alive, he feared that the anesthetic needed for the operation might kill them. Tanya countered by saying that less medication could be used in my case as I could take the pain – heaven knows that was true in all senses. The doctor was clearly pausing to reflect. Detecting some hesitation, Tanya let it be known that we were prepared to pay double. He replied that money was not a factor. In his professional opinion, what I wanted to have done was unnecessary for either tooth. He emphasized that all my teeth were in good condition and there was no sense in messing around with that. In fact, he went on to say, "I wouldn't do that to myself." (Я бы это себе не сделал).

No more needed to be said. I looked at the doctor's honest face, shook his hand, thanking him earnestly, and we marched out of there about as fast as we had entered. Case closed.

As soon as we found ourselves alone, urgently and impatiently, I turned to my lady. "OK, Tanya, the magic words, please: *what* did the Chief say?" She was sorry, she said. She had not been able to catch anything. I tried not to get angry and automatically assumed my scowling mode, wallowing in sheer disappointment. Damn it! Was I ever going to find out?

The Chief, anticipating that the dental work would take quite a while, had asked us to meet him in his office after the dentist's visit. So we returned to the Chief's place once more. As he was not there, Tanya suggested I wait for him while she inquired about the nearest grocery store. The Chief's secretary started explaining, but seeing Tanya's blank look, she got out of the building and explicitly pointed out where to go.

Tanya's close affair with grocery stores, the keepers of sustenance, goes back to rationed food in Soviet times. Her connection with food ranks higher than breathing air and all things sacred. Those were the days when people walked the streets with a "maybe bag" ("авоська,"), a netted bag one carried conveniently in their pockets hoping to get something, anything at all. During my stint as an International Research and Exchanges scholar in the early seventies, I saw people in Moscow and Leningrad standing in line, not knowing what they were waiting for.

Soon afterward, the Chief showed up, and his secretary informed him where Tanya had gone. "Follow me," he said as if issuing an order. He slid into his car and I into mine, and off we went. As if the devil was catching up with us, we vroomed to a street on the left, then to the right, and back to the left. We stopped suddenly in front of the store; he went in, found Tanya, and signaled to her that we were waiting outside.

When Tanya exited the store and got into my car, we followed the Chief again, racing to some farmhouse out of town where she could get some goat milk. -- Tanya tends to exploit proffered kindness long after it's been exhausted, and the Chief was no exception.

Ivan Victorovich was extremely helpful in every way. The time came to part ways, probably for all time. Given that I was the recipient of a tremendous amount of goodness and I'm the type who always strives to offer more than I receive, my problem was this: how do I reward such generosity of time, effort, and goodwill, especially under these circumstances? Tanya suggested I get him a bottle of balsam – an alcoholic drink made of various regional herbs, which I did. The Chief took it with an expression that was difficult to decipher. Did he expect something more or nothing? Without saying much, he matter-of-factly shot back to his duties while we, observing the speed limit now, drove to his dacha, where we had been spending the last two days.

The Chief had done all that driving around expensing his authority right and left out of the goodness of his heart. Tanya says it's the Belarusian way. People are good here, she insisted -- that's why they get pushed around and taken advantage of, she explained. The Chief's benevolence notwithstanding, chances are he wouldn't have acted the same way towards an unofficial Belarusian or Russian. However, Tanya claims my knowledge of Russian makes me one of their own ("свой"). This is convoluted logic at best. If the Chief wouldn't do it for one of their own, and if my Russian makes me one of their own, how come he still did it? In the end, Tanya opines it was because I'm an American. Honestly, I'm unable to wrap my mind around all of this. Here's a country where Americans, post-Afghanistan and Iraq, are still welcome! Is it because they dislike someone else more?

The day before, the Chief had proudly volunteered that his monthly salary was $400, four times that of a common laborer in this region! You might know that the median expected salary for a similar job in the States at this writing is about $8,000 monthly. I didn't have the heart to puncture the Chief's pride with that statistic. He volunteered that a pound of sausage cost about $3 here and wanted to know how much it costs in the States -- I guessed about twice as much. So, the Chief is at a significant disadvantage vis-à-vis his American counterpart. While his sausage may cost half of what it costs in America, his salary is 20 times less!

But does it really stop there?

Positively not! Comparisons of this kind are misleading. Other items, such as free education and medical care, or his house or taxes, which cost a fraction of what they do in America, would have to be included in the total picture. And so on.

So much for Burger-economics.

Evidently, sausage is an essential item here. I wondered if sausage might have been a more appropriate gift than balsam. But Tanya, my local expert, nixed the idea. I then thought of leaving him some money in the room, but Tanya firmly objected, stressing that it would be inappropriate. It does appear that the people here have more pride than money, which suits them just fine; thank you. The fact remains: they could use more money and less pride.

Ultimately, I was left scratching my head: Where can you make four doctor's visits in less than 30 minutes and without cost? I was still curious to know the magic words and how this feat had been achieved. I had tried to ease my gratitude aside, comprehend and interpret, as objectively as I could, what I had observed. I could see how the Chief employed his outstandingly commanding appearance and authority. But I sensed more went on behind the closed doors. I had been hoping Tanya's snooping would shed some light. Alas, it was not to pass!

Luck was not on my side, as it were. Tanya had only seen Ivan Victorovich whispering to the radiologist with his right hand cupped around his mouth and bending over close to the interlocutor's ear in a quasi-conspiratorial manner. But she was unable to capture the magic words. My disappointment grew as I felt an essential key to this entire experience was missing. My need to know grew as my desire to understand heightened my curiosity. *What did he say?* Whatever it was, the result was efficient and immediate line-cutting. Plain and simple. As an official, you can cut in, I surmised.

That this is not unlike what happens in other countries is not the point. For example, just a few days ago, hundreds of people in China were denied entry to a paid-for event due to the arrival of top Communist Party leaders. As soon as the people learned about it, they staged a three-hour-long mini-revolt: they blocked the officials from entering altogether, and the police and soldiers had to intervene.

Ivan Victorovich almost certainly did not break any rules on my behalf, as privileged treatment, a presumed perk of the powerful, has a long history in Soviet and post-Soviet societies. The fundamental point here is that it contradicts one's sense of fairness and equality. I couldn't help thinking that equality was one of the principal aims of the communist revolution. However pleasing to me, the Chief's preferential display mocked this notion of equality. It negated a cherished principle with absolute impunity. That it has long become the norm for the privileged class is a fact that drags this principle back full circle.

The second night was our last night at Ivan Victorovich's weird dacha room, where we were nevertheless fortunate to end up. But Ivan Victorovich was not done showering us with gentle, gentlemanly attention. In the early afternoon, dressed in civilian clothes, he visited us with two women amorously wrapped around his vast torso. His right hand rested over the younger woman's beautiful shoulder; his other hand was lost somewhere behind. He introduced them both as his former wives. Tanya maintained he was kidding, but he repeated the claim assertively and persuasively.

We sat on the wooden bench abutting the dacha. I brought out our small portable Yamaha, and Tanya played Tonkaya Ryabina (Тонкая Рябина, "rowan tree,") which she and I duetted with gusto. It's an old folk love song that can bring tears to emotionally starved souls. Our hosts loved it and praised my singing, ignoring Tanya's stellar performance. What really pleased them was perhaps not the quality of my musical output but that a foreigner was singing one of their own folk tunes with native feeling. We sang other songs and, leaving no room for objections, the Chief announced he would return later to take us to a banya (баня), his very own Belarusian bathhouse, for an experience to remember, he promised. His generosity mode was expanding.

A banya is typically a large structure, an ample sauna space, separate from the home, where one can get hot and then cold by going outside or jumping into a lake naked, sometimes in the presence of both men and women. I had mixed feelings; Tanya said she wanted to go but in her bathing suit. What the heck! I was game for the experience.

A couple of hours later, as agreed, Ivan Victorovich returned in the misty evening flanked by the same two dames we had met earlier. He asked us to follow them. Walking past some large bushes further down the hill from his dacha, we came up to a sizable log building. There was a big wooden table out front with two substantial wooden benches on either side; the whole assembly was outdoors but covered by a roof.

Tanya and I sat against the banya wall to protect ourselves from the falling evening temperature. For good measure and without warning, and despite the fact she grew up in subarctic Murmansk, she grabbed my jacket. She put it over her shoulders, defeating my plan to keep my southern European-born-and-raised body warm. She may not be selfish but acts like it sometimes, leaving you no choice. As her man, you want to be a gentleman but risk freezing to death while trying to keep warm according to whatever wisdom you've picked up during your earthly existence. Clearly, you do not control your body's warm comfort with her.

While inside the banya, we experienced the expected severe sweating. You and your partner alternate beating each other's bodies with wet birch branches to stimulate blood circulation and do whatever else the activity may afford. Ivan Victorovich went in first with Tatyana, his younger former wife. There were some better left-undescribed sounds. Tanya and I went in after the Chief and his companion came out.

Our giant host invited us to follow him when we finished with the banya. He led the way by straddling the used tires strewn onto the swampy ground. Past the last large bush, a placid body of dark water thrust itself into our eyes in the moonlight. Without wasting any time, Ivan Victorovich plunged into the lake; he urged us to jump in. The ladies declined, but hero me stuck his big right toe into the cold water and hesitated. The Chief, who had served in the Soviet Bearing Sea Navy, urged me on. I wanted to oblige, and I might have even wanted to impress the ladies. Motivated by Napoleonic bravado and skipping the presumably protective crossing of myself, I plunged into the frigid water, feeling my lungs heaving rapidly and deeply. For a moment, I wondered if my breathing was going to stop. But hardly a few minutes had passed when I felt elevated to apotheotic awareness – I was no longer cold! My breathing had normalized, and I experienced the joy of being fully alive, a healthy being in an unfathomable dark body of water during a dimly-lit Belarusian night.

After a while, we returned to the banya. We sat at the outdoor bench by the front of the bathhouse and sampled a fair array of goodies. We had brought lots of beer, but it did not get touched. There was samogon (самогон, "moonshine"), a local high-proof liquor. There was a great salad, home-made pickled cucumbers, and kvas (квас), a fermented drink so typical of the Slavs. As if that were not enough, Ivan Victorovich proceeded al fresco to cook skewered chicken that tasted out of this world. I enjoyed every morsel of it. There were a lot of discussions. I felt like one of them and was led and let to believe it was so. A tremendous human experience: if you catch yourself forgetting your "otherness" in a foreign country, make sure you acknowledge to whom credit belongs.

I forced the discussion on issues about Belarus and the Belarusian character. I was on a roll. I got up and, going around the big wooden table, eased myself next to the Chief. Feeling forever minuscule next to his mountainous bulk, I hardened my spirit. I really wanted to scream: *what were the damn magic words, Chief?* How were you able to bend people's wills so shamelessly and easily? But instead, I voiced the burning question in as friendly and casual a tone as possible and finally got my answer.

A hot Belarusian sweaty sauna, potent moonshine, incomparable camaraderie, and a cold lake night plunge, without a doubt, not only enhanced the exquisite food's flavor but also helped to loosen the Chief's tongue, allowing the magic words to finally flow out:

"We've got one from the ministry here." (Тут один из министерства.)

Note: All names used in this story are fictitious.
Pullman, Washington
August 2012

My First Memory

"They're killing us!!!" My mother cried. With my younger sister in her arms, I see her scramming away from our house in complete panic. I'm scampering as fast as I can, a few steps behind. I hear the hum of bombers overhead. I can see them; they're not very high.

This is my life's first memory ever, and it is one of mortal fear!

"Grigora! Grigora!" (Hurry up!) "Bombs, bombs! They're killing us; hurry up!!!" My mother had yanked me from my bed only moments earlier as if I were an empty sack. She had never acted like that before. Why was she so rough with me this morning?

"Bombs, bombs, hurry up!" she was repeating. I had heard that word for the first time a few days earlier. I didn't know what it meant, but I remember my mother saying, "The Italians are killing us." My mother's words were forcefully inscribing a brand-new concept into my consciousness.

Italians-bombs-killing.

The association stuck. I understood; I sensed extreme, life-threatening danger. An armor of fear enveloped me, and I just stood there as if petrified. My mother screamed, "We're going to the Zervases now! Run, run!"

Zervas was our closest neighbor on the south side. An empty field and a small vineyard separated our houses.

In my mind's eye, I can still see my mother scurrying out of the house, trying to run her fastest. I sense she's highly agitated, frightened, and horrified. She's in total panic. In her left hand, she's holding my younger sister, still a toddler, and a checkered woolen blanket -- I can still see its black and red squares.

"Grigora, grigora!" (Hurry up!) she shouts, rushing as fast as possible. My little sister is beginning to cry louder and louder. My mother isn't paying any attention to her or me. She hurriedly stuffs some things in a bag, grabs it with her right hand, and, not bothering to close the door, hits the road running, her eyes fixed on some void before her. We're rushing uphill towards the neighbor's house, a couple hundred yards away. I can't keep up with her. The distance separating us is growing. My mother's terror grips my being like a runaway electrical current. I feel panic-stricken, and I begin to cry, too.

"Mama, mama, perimene!" (Wait!).

We reach the neighbor's place, and my mother turns left. We run some more. Someone is calling out:

"Elate edo" (over here). It's a voice from inside the ground, as if from a grave. She steps down some earthen steps, and I follow, catching up. We are in a rectangular hole in the earth -- a homemade bomb shelter. It's like a large grave dug with earthen seats on either side. Several people are already seated facing each other. Large logs with hay and leaves form the roof close above our heads. My mother takes a seat on the left row and pushes me to her left. To my left, I see Zervas, our giant neighbor; other members of his family and other neighbors fill out the rest of the space. A recent yelling dispute between my mother and a neighbor sitting opposite her has vanished into thin air. The common danger, it seems, has united us all in this hole here and now.

No one is talking. People are horror-stricken; they look strange to me and seem to look past each other as if at some looming object in the distance.

The Italian aerial attacks on Patras, the third-largest city in Greece, took place in October 1940. Our home was in the suburbs. Italian biplanes flew over our house, heading toward downtown Patras, seven kilometers east. In my mind's ear, I can still hear the hum of their engines. I see two planes flying close together, then another, followed by two more. Several more were to follow.

Bombs rained in densely populated areas – many people were killed. According to eyewitnesses, blood was everywhere, limbs were thrown around, bodies were decapitated without arms or legs, and people were screaming and crying. A bus loaded with people caught fire. Electrical poles and lines fell to the ground, instilling fear of electrocution. Veritable pandemonium.

Why were these innocent citizens, going about their daily lives, targeted? Who decided to do this and why? Who gave the right or permission for such an atrocity? Why? Why? It makes no sense.

This was at the beginning of the Second World War. Hitler's killing machine spills blood further and further from the Third Reich. War, mass slaughter, desolation, misery, and wretchedness reign supreme -- mass killers are at work. A lot of damage, man-made and avoidable, is being done to civilization. Man's worst cruelty to man has been unleashed. Mass murderers appear to be competing in excelling in violence --cruel, idiotic humanity in action. It's wartime. Again!

Italy's Benito Mussolini joined his country's murder capability with Hitler's killing machine. Mussolini launched an unprovoked and treacherous attack on our city before the ultimatum had expired. Our town was subjected to massive aerial attacks, and innocent blood flowed in the streets aplenty.

If I owe my life's first horrific memory to Mussolini, he owes his horrifying death to Divine Justice. Five years later, he got his comeuppance – he was shot dead and hung for all to see.

I was two and a half years old. How old were you when you had your first memory, and was it pleasant?

Recent research has shown that people's first memory is at about that age on average. In some cases, based on parents' recollections, some first memories have occurred at an even younger time of life. As we grow old, we reset the past time closer to our current time, so we don't have a real sense of the time of occurrence. However, to establish my own first memory, I know when I was born and when the bombing took place. It's not possible to reset those days.

Two-and-a-half years old is a very tender age. Having such a rude awakening by any standard is a challenging time. I recall it as if it were almost yesterday, so profoundly it must have been engraved in my child's mind. It is said that traumatic experiences burn lasting memories even at the earliest age. Two and a half years old qualifies in my case. This must be my earliest memory, with sadder ones to follow.

People never learn war's true meaning; they seem programmed for it. All it takes is a "Fuehrer," and like dangerous sheep, off they go – slaughtering and getting slaughtered. It's too late when they finally learn their lesson, as the damage has already been done. They return a generation or two later, off to another war. People's passions run wild; their memories are short, and wisdom is scarce.

What do you think "civilized society" means? Is it art, architecture, music, dance, literature, etc.? We find all that in war and peace, even in non-life. The basic concept of what a civilized society should be is not that complex. One can start with mutual respect -- we recognize people's rights and space, respect them, and expect people to reciprocate. Simple! There shouldn't be any room for cruelty in a civilized society, a very fragile entity. Intelligent people recognize the importance of stamping out infractions from the start. Significant conflicts, like wars, start with minor transgressions. It's paramount to be vigilant and take action promptly to safeguard our civilized modus vivendi. This is the temple it's worthwhile to light a candle to.

∞∞∞∞

If we more or less agree on what a civilized society should be, how difficult would it be to ensure it becomes a reality? Don't tell me that others have struggled with this before or question who I think I am to presume whatever. That others confronted this issue means they recognized the problem. That they failed or partially succeeded should not discourage us from trying again. Simply put, a solution is called for if the issue remains unsolved.

There are plenty of worthwhile areas to devote our energies to; we have a severe problem as a dominant living entity on this earth. For good reasons, we invest much time in various issues affecting our planet and its ecosystems. Isn't the human ecosystem the most important for all of us? Where are our priorities? Are we devoid of enough wisdom to order our issues and proceed accordingly?

Why do we spend so much time shutting our eyes to the truth? Why do we allow controlling but controllable forces to guide us away from universal good? Why are we investing so much energy in evil? Why do we allow large-scale corruption amongst us in the first place? Where's the power and authority to deal with evil, recognize and control it? Why is it more critical to ensure a deterrent when the solution would be to eliminate the need for it in the first place?

As I observe nature stumbling across repeated patterns, one thing is clear: living things live and die, one species feeding on another. The invasive trait is only fueled by a loss of control. Every species wants to predominate, but nature does provide controls. Can we not learn from nature's example? Natural and unnatural deaths, plagues, diseases, pandemics, and natural disasters exist. Where's nature's control over people's evil doing? If it were likened to a parasite living off other organisms, one wonders why we haven't, as a species, found a definitive way to deal with it? Why do we let chance dictate our fate as a people? Why do we allow evil-propagating notions in our midst? Why do we need armies for territorial rights when we should focus on extinguishing territorial separators?

Why are we powerless to deal with the root of problems but find all sorts of means to focus on symptoms? Witness how much genius has gone and is going into nuclear technology. Would it take more intellect to focus on the preservation of peace instead?

Suppose I allowed myself to offer some kind of a solution. Why not consider an *international force with teeth*? You would quickly point out the United Nations and all of that. If I focused on the "teeth" part, you might mention the Blue Helmets, a United Nations army of sorts.

OK. I agree there's all that, but it has no real teeth. I will also agree that there's no originality in any of my subsumed proposals here. But I will insist that while all that may be correct, *a comprehensive solution with teeth needs to be implemented.* At the risk of being labeled simple-minded, I will add that the problem ipso facto is not complicated or hard to see. It's people who make it so. As we develop ways to control invasive plants, why can't we do likewise with invasive human behavior?

We need guaranteed world peace. The world has never been assured of a foolproof and comprehensive banning of armed conflict. Bands of belligerents can rise anywhere and very often do. A constant Damocle's Sword hangs over the lives of millions of people anytime, anywhere.

I envision a Global Superagency comprised of members chosen from among the wisest of all humans to guide us and protect our peace. Its first edict would prohibit the use of all weapons of mass destruction.

I envision a Global Superforce with the mandate and complete authority to collect and dispose of all weapons of war and to prevent armed conflict anywhere and at any time. While countries could establish courts and maintain police forces for law and order only, their number and arsenal would be entirely subservient to the Global Superforce.

This is as simple a concept as it gets, and what's there to disagree about? Would psychopathic leaders be able to do what has happened throughout history, including today? Would there have been a Hitler and the like?

I'm grateful I survived to have my first memory at all. How many children will not!

Boquete, Panama
February 2022

Springtime in Greece. It's 1941. A year and a half earlier, Germany started The Second World War, the world's most destructive war ever known. By this time, Germany controlled most of continental Europe and, with its Axis allies, prepared to invade the Soviet Union. In March of that year, Winston Churchill, Prime Minister of England, relocated 58,000 British and Australian forces from Egypt to Greece to delay the German advance. Many British troops arrived at the Peloponnese, and some landed on Rio's beach.

Rio, a suburb of Patras, Greece's third-largest city, is my birthplace; I spent the first 18 years of my life there. My early years were marred by the Italian and German occupations, the stationing of British forces, and the Greek Civil War.

I vividly recall three or four British soldiers eating lunch on our beach one day. I see my brother and myself in my mind's eye, intently walking toward them. From a discrete distance, we look at these newcomers with profound interest. My child's mind registers my observations — how they opened their ration cans, what the cans contained, and more. My brother and I squatted on the pebbly beach, ogling the soldiers as if they were visitors from another planet.

Their can rations were likely of greater interest to us at that food scarcity time.

Munching their food and chatting, the soldiers ravenously consumed their rations. They then helped themselves to what I now presume might have been biscuits and chocolate.

The soldiers paid no heed to us, but we found them quite interesting. Looking at all the goodies, our eyes opened their hungriest wide, which must have been noticed. One of the soldiers, facing us, whispered something to his companions, who immediately focused their attention on us. The soldier then got up and approached us, offering a bar of chocolate with a broad smile.

Excitedly, I grabbed it and pressed it to my chest with both hands as if it were a prized possession or trophy. Then, I proceeded to make my way home in great exhilaration. My brother, a bit older than I, rushed after me; he unceremoniously clutched the chocolate off my hands and was about to run off with it until the soldiers perceived the goings-on. One of them strode over, speaking sternly in a language we could not understand.

Unthreateningly, he placed his hand on my perplexed brother's shoulder, and with his free hand, he reached for the chocolate – he broke it in two halves and gave each of us one half.

There! That's how civilized people do it.

We train our soldiers to kill and somehow believe they can turn their learned killing faculty on and off at will and with wisdom. But how do we give them the ability to make that choice, especially in the field? We expect them to return someday to the life they left behind -- their family and friends -- to incorporate themselves again into society and, most importantly, behave. How do they "unlearn" this training once they are released back to "civilized society?" Do we hope some trace of reformative humanity is left in them?

War is not for civilized people, although so-called civilized people always originate it. Our civilized societies turn to savage behavior in the blink of an eye, brutalizing their neighbors. What is needed to make us so if we are not genuinely civilized?

My brother crunched his chocolate share impatiently, licking the last crumb off his fingers and lips. By contrast, being of the save-for-later kind, I bit off a tiny piece, savoring it to prolong its gratifying effect. The sweet taste filled my heart with awe and gratitude for my good fortune.

Why with gratitude? Does food taste better when eaten with thankfulness? Do things go better with gratefulness? Perhaps, but this was likely my first chocolate ever, and, truth be told, it is my favorite sweet to this day.

Can you tell an expression of gratitude on someone's face? Do you know how your eyes or the rest of your face put that expression together? Perhaps not, but I hope you know how it feels to be grateful, express gratitude, and receive it. Gratitude is a much more significant concept than most people realize. It can generate many good feelings and actions; it's a good motivator -- a precious tool in the arsenal of human goodness.

The next day, we returned to the beach hoping for chocolate seconds, only to find that the soldiers and their massive vessel were nowhere to be seen. Looking wistfully at the offing and the sea beyond, we ambled along the shore, somewhat disheartened, keenly wishing for the soldiers to return.

Unmindful of man's fortunes, mopping the seawater like gigantic brushes, the waves were doing what they have always done -- they coaxed anything in their path untiringly against the shore.

One oblong object caught my attention; I had seen or recognized nothing familiar. It was something new for four-year-old me. I picked it up with reverence; it was soaking wet, but I liked the feel of its ring. I pulled at its ends -- it stretched. My practical mind felt the joy of discovery – I thought the immense sea had sent me a toy! This was shaping into a fantastic day, first the chocolate and now this! Life is good.

In war-soaked Greece, my siblings and I did not have toys. Even the concept was alien to me. But the desire to have toys, to toy with something, was not. Children and even adults need toys. It's not uncommon for children with no toys to make their own and use their imagination, moving them around in various ways. By bending junk wire a few years later, I recall how I built what I believed was a bus. My mother admired it and enjoyed showing it to our restaurant customers. I relished demonstrating its powerful engine sound, which, of course, I provided on the spot.

Playing is a necessary and therapeutic occupation – we're somehow pre-wired for it by nature. We do something analogous with words; have you noticed?

However, my "beach toy" was not of my own making; I thought it was something I found on the beach -- a gift from the sea. I proudly showed it to my brother. My bourgeoning imagination had promptly provided a couple of innocuous scenarios with this toy. My brother wasted no time snatching it from my hands, and after examining it briefly, he hurled it back into the sea as far as he could. I got angry at him as he thwarted my efforts to enjoy my newly-found toy. War or not, some kind of life goes on, and at that moment, all that mattered to me was my toy – I had no concept of war or peace.

My brother liked flinging things as far as possible; he was proud of his javelin strength. I suppose that was one way of fostering his sense of muscular preeminence and keeping others feeling subservient and pliable.

However, the Good Fairy, or perhaps Goddess Aphrodite, was looking out for me. Further, down the beach, I spotted another "toy," just like the first one. Without alerting my brother, I ran to pick it up. I grabbed it from its ring, full of joyful anticipation; I noticed it changing shape because of the liquid within. I turned it over in my fingers and liked its smooth softness. I held it upside down, and the liquid poured off.

Aphrodite, the Ancient Greek Mythology goddess of beauty and non-brotherly love, by one account, was said to have emerged at a remote Cyprus beach from the foam of the waves. (Years later, believe it or not, I actually went there.) Aphrodite, or Venus, as the Romans would call her, was the sea's gift to my ancient procreative progenitors. Indeed, just like my beach toy, she was a present from the sea, don't you see?

As is commonly known, children love putting things in their mouths. Some adults do, too, undoubtedly. So, I brought the toy to my lips and blew air into it. To my surprise, it held the air well – aha! Mystery solved – it's a balloon! Secure in knowing that I had found an actual balloon, off I ran, my brother in tow. I brought it home and proudly displayed its inflated magnificence like a gonfalon high above my head. I ran circles around my coveting brother and sisters -- I was finally celebrating a "real toy" in the sideyard of our house. But my joy was fated for a short life when my mother saw the spectacle.

Έλα δω, ρε! (Come here, you!), my mother yelled, rushing over; she snatched the balloon from my hands and summarily disposed of it in the toilet while spouting a torrent of unkind words. In an instant, she returned, practically frothing at the mouth, rushed to the kitchen, and quickly returned with a soapy wet rag. She scrubbed my lips, mouth, and hands with powerful strokes as if to extirpate a plague. And for good measure, she granted my brother the same treatment, although he hadn't even touched the offending balloon.

This felt like a great injustice to me.

After all, I had no toys, not even a balloon; my parents had never given my siblings or me any toys. Now that some benevolent force graced me with a toy, absolutely my own, and I was enjoying it, my mother bizarrely yanked it away. Where's the justice in that? Little did it help that she would not bother to explain why she was so troubled and what it was all about.

I felt violated and powerless. Even terrorized. How would any four-year-old feel? What did my siblings think, and what did they learn from that?

I walked off feeling like a brick had suddenly hit my head. I went to our bedroom and buried my face in the bed my brother and I shared. Bewildered and despairing, I sobbed loudly, pounding the mattress with my tiny fists. I was distraught and fuming with feelings of hatred contaminating my four-year-old heart. First, my brother tossed my first find back into the sea, and now my mother has thrown my second one into the sewer. Why couldn't I have toys? What was so sinful about playing? My negative emotions from this experience blistered my mind for years to come.

Lest you misjudge my mother's reaction, let me rush to her defense. The fact is, an undeniably totally uncommon event suddenly exploded in front of her like a grenade. Chances are, she panicked! Her response was probably instinctive and driven by motherhood, culture, and family honor. Family honor has been a compelling concept in the world I grew up in. I now surmise that my sisters' presence may have beclouded my mother's mind to the exclusion of much else. It's another matter that she didn't segue with a tranquil and educational chat with me, with all of us children. Times change, and identical situations may require different handling, leading to other consequences. My mother, blessed be her soul, did her best considering the circumstances. I, therefore, pronounce her wholly blameless.

My negative emotions are no longer blazing in my mind; instead, in permanent oblivion, they've joined my first toy down the unfeeling latrine. Paradoxically, it took only an instant for my first toy, the sea's present to me, to vanish forever. Yet, lovely Aphrodite, the sea's illustrious gift to humanity, has endured for all time.

Boquete, Panama
January 2022

My First Love

Rio de Janeiro may throw the world's most famous Carnival parades. Nevertheless, my Greek hometown, Rio-Patras, can likewise brag about its own. Like Rio de Janeiro, Patras, probably the third-largest city in Greece, throws its own feral street celebration with gigantic floats, masks, and forgivable wantonness once a year from mid-January to mid-February.

My Rio lies on the outskirts of Patras. While the Carnival floats do not flood Rio itself, the Carnival frolickers undoubtedly do. Once a year, pleasure-seeking people from all over Greece descend upon Patras to participate in this show of fake madness. And they need a place to stay. Father's hotel would quickly fill up those days, and so would all available beds in the vicinity at unusually exorbitant prices.

During this pagan/Christian holiday, my first erotic love made landfall upon my then 15-year-old existence. The year was 1953. Like a hurricane, it uprooted and swirled me violently into a new and unfamiliar world. Powered by my runaway imagination and explosive sexuality, my love gained volume and strength, overtaking my reason. Come rain or Vorias, the mighty Akrotiri wind, I'd hop on my bicycle and ride several kilometers to where Antonia lived and worked in the hope of catching a glimpse of her. I would do that twice a day!

Antonia Mouxa, a charming lass of about my age, worked as a domestic for the Koulis family, a better-to-do family occupying the director's quarters at Restis, the then-newly established oil refinery by the seashore nearby. Antonia's multi-member family lived in one of the suburban communities not far from there.

During the Patras Carnival (Καθαρή Δευτέρα, Κούλουμα), people would go out to taverns or restaurants to eat skewered meat, listen to traditional Greek music, gossip, dance a little, and simply ogle each other. Father's eatery was then one of Rio's scarce megaphone music sources.

The Koulis family was among the customers who came to our restaurant that fateful Carnival Monday, bringing Antonia along. Antonia danced a lot and rather well. I recall her elegant figure perfectly emphasizing every root beat of the traditional dances. I can still see her beautiful face singing along with seductively guileful abandon. Her natural grace captured my eye and ignited my love right away. I was yanked off my foundation; I became airborne.

Have you ever wondered what the difference between sanity and madness is? Don't crazy people sometimes behave rationally?

I was not mad if madness meant a passing fever, but I was impregnated with passion. Passionate by nature, romantic by character, and stuffed with the reading of novels, made me a victim of myself, who I was, and where I was headed. My passion was alive and dominant. It was a considerable, impossible-to-ignore entity inside me, an entrenched domineering companion that never left me. No decision could be made without its interference. It owned me, possessed me, led me, and was my master. I have no idea what it must have done to my blood pressure, but I could feel the river of blood pulsating powerfully within.

I set out to conquer this ethereal female. I began riding my bicycle regularly along the beach a couple of miles away from our home. I would go no further than the refinery entrance. From there, I would snoop the house in the hope of seeing and being seen by her. I made a note in my diary of the time I saw her and of the time I thought she had noticed me. I can still see her with my mind's eye as she exited the house, walked down a few steps along the side, and then disappeared right back inside.

One cold-weather day, I braved the bicycle ride as usual in the hope of making contact. The wind was so icy and robust that, my solid teenage legs notwithstanding, it proved almost impossible to pedal my way further. I forged ahead on foot, pushing my bicycle with great effort. As no sighting took place, I returned later that same day in the evening, alas once again failing to see her. With every passing day, forever wallowing in hopeful disappointment, I was weaving a volcanic romance in my mind. I recall how I'd visualize the two of us picnicking under some majestic pine trees in the forest nearby, me playing Schubert's serenade exclusively for her on the violin. This picture is still vivid in my mind -- only for some reason, I appear to be considerably taller in my mind.

Antonia's physical shape became the prototype for several women in my subsequent love life – a pretty, coquettish face reigning over a slender, elegant, statuesque body. I had found my goddess. It's pointless arguing whether her shape and grace may have been the prototype of beauty that had been in my head all along.

I was desperately desirous of making contact. I was convinced Antonia was equally interested in me and felt emboldened to intensify my courting.

As the days passed, my passion blinded me enough to write a confession of love to her and place it where she could find it. This was the kind of love, more splendid than life itself, which only a super-passionate fifteen-year-old can engender. Although not a single word had been exchanged between us, our imagined relationship snowballed in my mind's fertile soil. I was convinced Antonia reciprocated entirely, and I waited eagerly for our first encounter. There remained no doubt in my mind that the attraction and love were utterly mutual.

It's interesting to note how our mind becomes our ally and accomplice whenever passion rules.

My concept of love was much more platonic than any subsequent amorous hallucinations. I had an immense well of pure love to share, to join my fate with my chosen person of the opposite sex for the rest of my life. This desire has flourished in me ever since I can remember. In its most idealistic version, it even included beatific delusions of self-sacrifice at the temple of my beloved. I felt the conflict between the physical and the mental part of love fiercely battling within my adolescent body. My fiery imagination rode my blood flow hard and made it throb wildly. My witnessing of couples enjoying an afternoon fix at our little hotel and the murkiness of my unfathomable sexuality led to battling vivid fantasies with female schoolmates for as long as I can remember. I couldn't prevent this involuntary fantasizing even with Mary the Virgin during the liturgy in Church! This caused me much chagrin as I had been raised in a deeply religious environment. I felt miserably sinful and guilty before mighty heaven.

The battle lines were drawn, and the forces of religion and youthful, unbridled passion raging inside me were waging war.

As an adult striving to understand, I can only blame my nature. I suspect all this was normal, that I was not exceptional. But it was unique to me then, and in my own world, there was only me. This physical/mental passion duo ruled and nearly ruined my life. It became my Golgotha. While besieged by irrepressible forces inside me, I spent a lifetime clinging loyally to the ideas of marriage and family. This struggle left me empty and unrequited -- I had been looking for the unattainable, nay, the non-existent.

When does passion turn into desire?

I kept up my visits to the factory entrance, hoping to get a response from the bold letter of my love confession. I suppose I was driven by instinct.

The power of instinct is inexorable. It's fortunate when instinct coincides with logic. But frequently, it does not. Have you ever seen how some birds, pecking tirelessly on a windowpane against their own reflection, engage in utterly headstrong behavior? They most likely engage in a mortal battle for territorial rights against what they consider a threatening opponent. I recall a mockingbird knocking its beak against its own windowpane reflection and ending up moribund on my patio.

The days were slipping slowly by as my passion grew like a volcano inside me. I composed a poetic letter in my mind and was planning to proceed. I was in love limbo. I don't know how long this lasted, but I wondered if there would ever be an encounter. Without warning, the day of the fateful encounter did indeed come. But it was an encounter of the wrong kind, whose effect has lasted to this day.

As I was riding homeward after one of my regular exploratory outings, I became aware of a bicycle rider overtaking me to my right. "Can I borrow your pump for a minute?" he asked me expectantly. I turned to see who it was and realized it was my beloved's older brother. I did not know what to think, and of course, I stopped right away, eagerly proffering my pump. If I had any inkling of what was to follow, I could have glanced at his tires and taken appropriate action. But I felt anxious to help a future relative.

As soon as he got my bicycle pump, he began hitting me repeatedly and rhythmically in silence as if he were performing some mystic ritual. This was a real beating. I can still hear the pump's thudding against my raised arms and its clanking against itself. Yes, there was some bleeding. When he felt he was done, he simply handed me the pump and went his way -- mission accomplished. I had just been served a brutal massage and a stern message.

I managed to get back on my bicycle. I took a less frequented path back home, totally confused, humiliated, and profoundly disappointed, yet fully aware of the delivered lesson. I did not want to ride past the shops and the small public square in my deplorable condition. Like a wounded bull, I rode straight home, and without stopping at my usual spot in the front of the house, I rode as quickly as I could to the back, where the children's bedroom was. I hit the bed face down and began wailing uncontrollably. Fortunately, no one in the family noticed anything, as they were all busy with their chores at the other end of the big house. The physical pain was the least of my troubles -- I was not paying any attention to my physical wounds. My heart was filled with deep disappointment and despair. I was now weeping but wanted to sob, my chest heaving with emotion; I wanted to howl but had to keep quiet. The profound mourning of my lost first love had begun in earnest. I remember this very clearly.

I have no idea how long I lay there, allowing my emotions to regain some semblance of balance. I had been betrayed -- my great love had betrayed me, and I had been beaten cruelly to boot. I was hurting within and without. I was bleeding without and within. I would never see her, nor would I ever get to talk to her for all time. My first great love had unexpectedly come to a very abrupt, painful, and miserable end. I felt sure I would never love again. I locked the incident hermetically inside me, as my shame and pride wouldn't allow me to share it with anyone until now.

Time went by as I licked my wounds and reflected upon my fate. More than once in the following days, I wondered if life was worth living after such a sad denouement. I had been initiated into the momentous game of love in complete innocence; some of that innocence was now permanently lost. I swore I'd never love again but quickly arrived at a philosophical accommodation. I told myself I had been merely fishing -- one could spend indefinite periods never knowing whether there would be a fish. Sometimes, the catch would even have to be thrown back into the water.

I soon realized that life was worth living as further female fantasizing and experiences eagerly repaired all damage.

Sometimes, life handles relationships in surprising and even mystifying ways. Was it proper for me to get that beating? Was it fair? I knew who the man was, and he knew who I was. He was an adult, and I was a 15-year-old kid. We had no relationship – we were members of the same community. An accidental encounter with his kid sister led to a youthful infatuation, which resulted in a noble pubescent courtship culminating with my written confession of love. Should I have been forgiven my impertinence with a scolding and a warning, or was that brutal physical punishment the only way? Did the culture demand the latter? No, definitely not. I recall an analogous instance with a young man from our community. He expressed his intense attraction for my oldest sister with a blind passion more than once. My parents and his found a peaceful way to control him. There was no beating.

Whether life *intends* to teach us a lesson can be disputed, but what is clear is that the experience itself does constitute the lesson. The incident did affect me significantly, but it may have also affected both Antonia and her brother, whom my actions made unwitting participants. As my successes in life became known in their community, it's reasonable to assume that the siblings may have had second thoughts and even regrets. After returning from the United States to Greece to see my dying father, who desperately needed a blood transfusion, I unexpectedly encountered my first love's brother, my beater, in my father's living room! As our eyes met, his face lit up with a meaningful smile.

"Με θυμάσαι;" (Do you remember me?) he asked me softly. It took me a bit to place him even after he timidly uttered his name, as 29 years had passed since he had savaged me with my bicycle pump on that fateful day. I smiled back, first in a condescending way, then in a friendly manner, and finally in a grateful way.

The man had come to offer my dying father his own blood!

Pullman, Washington
September 2017

The Flag Caper

After German, Italian, and Bulgarian occupiers left its soil in 1945, Greece wasted no time opening its schools. Since elementary education was compulsory, all eligible ages had to comply. And as the school opening coincided with my age eligibility – I was just the right age for first grade – I lucked out. However, all the children held back during the Second World War years would be in the same one-room schoolroom together. Thus, I found myself with students 4-5 years my senior. Thanks to my enthusiasm and rapid progress, I quickly became the teacher's pet.

One of the older students, Christos, who had proved to be a bully and troublemaker, could always be relied upon to stir things up. During the sixth grade, he and some other older students entertained themselves by setting my brother and me against another pair of brothers over a fabricated pretext. This resulted in after-school fistfights, which occurred over several weeks. But Christos had other, more ambitious plans.

The three-year Greek Civil War ended in 1949. The country began moving on, and trucks played an important role. Small commemorative flags were popular on trucks at that time. They symbolized a nation celebrating the end of a horrific era that followed the power vacuum created by the Second World War. Vehicles had to overnight at Father's hotel to wait for the next day's ferry to take them across the Rion-Antirrion straights. Christos figured they were an easy target. He conceived of a plan to steal all the flaglets one night. Some neighborhood kids were recruited for the nocturnal operation. A schoolmate and I were told to watch and warn if anyone approached while Christos and his buddies removed the little flags. The plan was executed without a hitch.

The next day, even before the spoils got distributed amongst the perpetrators, the truck drivers noticed the absence of their colorful flags. The police were alerted and began their investigation without delay. They interviewed all the neighborhood kids and immediately found out what had happened. They came to our restaurant and asked to talk to my brother and me. I shared all I knew, which they already knew. They told my parents they needed to take me to the police station. *Was I under arrest?*

A policeman walked me to the central police station a few miles away in the next community. During the 30-minute trek, he asked me various questions, and I took advantage of the opportunity to make a good impression. He asked me about the school, and I didn't fail to brag about my achievements. I told him I had always gotten "arista," the highest diploma grade. Also, the year before, the teacher gave me parts in four school plays, more than anyone else, because she liked my performance! Evidently, I knew how to make a good impression -- even good kids make mistakes here and there, was the idea.

"I want you to pay attention to what happens to bad people," the policeman said as we approached the police station.

Like out of an overfilled cup, fear began spilling out of my child's soul, releasing turbulent chemical reactions throughout my sensitive being. *My God, what had I gotten into!*

I saw Christos in a kneeling posture outside the police station. His bare knees, supporting all his weight, were lightly bleeding on a thin pile of small, sharp, crushed rock pieces. His hands were tied behind his back, and his eyes were shamefully fixed on the ground. I was led past him and into the house slowly and ceremoniously. The policeman made sure I took in the show.

"Behold the thief-in-chief," he said for all to hear as if uttering a well-prepared phrase. I was next taken to the balcony on the other side; my hands were placed on the railing, and a string was loosely tied around them. I could easily have pulled my hands back, but I left them exactly where the policeman had placed them. I was in extreme repentance mode. I feared my punishment was coming next.

My fear was soon succeeded by a sense of profound humiliation. I remember a passenger train passing by while I was standing "tied" at the balcony railing. I thought all eyes were nailed on my shame. This image is still vivid in my mind. After a short while, the policeman returned and removed the string. With my eyes nailed to the ground, and I imagine my face white with terror, I prepared myself for my deserved castigation. However, after admonishing me never to do anything wrong again, the policeman let me go without further ado. After receiving a slap on the wrist, a minor reprimand suitable for my misdeed, I strutted out like a child, anxious to be re-incorporated into the family home sweet home.

Indeed, when I returned home, my mother was waiting impatiently for me.

" Έλα εδώ, κατεργάρη!." (Come here, you rascal!) she said, violently grabbing my right wrist with her left hand while holding a hefty stick with the other. She marched me to our community's public square. It's there that she unleashed her formidable anger and indignation. In her exaggerated estimation, although I had not received anything from the theft spoils, I had shamed our family by participating as a watchperson in the flaglet caper. She started beating me hard while verbalizing her lesson for all to hear. She even made sure everyone, including those inside the main café, noticed her loud yells; they came out to enjoy the show. She may have thought she was doing the right thing, especially protecting the family's honor. She was a good soldier in duty performance mode.

My psychological anguish masked any and all physical pain. It felt as if my world was coming to an end. I desperately needed a place to hide.

When she felt she was done, she let go of my hand in disgust and indignation.

"Να, ρε κερατά." (There you go, you rascal.) She sighed as if washing her hands off after a dirty task. I was not a person in all this; I was an object used to satisfy my mother's community image requirements. Despite my condition, I also detected some strange pride in her demeanor. In her estimation, she had performed her duty admirably -- see, this is what a proper mother should do!

I followed her home like a severely beaten dog with its tail between its hind legs. My wounded heart did not want that mother. I wanted to be far away from her and from it all.

How can filial love survive such treatment?

As I had been at the police station, I had not had lunch that day. My mother made sure there was no dinner for me either.

The police had treated me humanely, but had my mother?

I was 11 years old.

∞∞∞∞

I went to school the next day. The class was studying algebraic proportions. All went as normal until the teacher addressed himself to me peremptorily:

"Ο κλέφτης στον πίνακα τώρα!" (The thief to the blackboard now!) I was still smarting from my mother's cruelty. The shaming had now morphed into an extreme insult and public ridicule. Upon hearing the teacher's offensive remark, my mind became highly clouded. I stood before the blackboard, petrified in utter shame and confusion. Any remaining sense of self-worth was demolished at that moment. From a top student, I was, as if by evil magic, reduced to a failure. My performance for that teacher never recovered. Fortunately, it was my first and last year with him. However, this damage was to be carried on to mathematics in particular. Although I was good at math, it took years to recover. In fact, I have not healed completely, as a minor psychological block still lingers when dealing with simple algebraic ratio problems.

My mother's cruel punishment of me had become the talk of the town by the next day and may have inspired the teacher to continue the abuse of me. Whatever my mother's good intentions and motivation, she did more harm than good. She had put my shame on the community's front page for all to see; I became the town's scorn. Her action singled me out, turning me into the community's free for all target -- from the police and family to the public and school: I was regally traumatized. The physical damage was no ongoing problem, but the psychological blow was severe, not only because of my wounded pride but also because of the injustice of it all. I lost my stellar classroom standing. I became less of myself, suppressed and depressed.

I don't recall any public shaming for the other kids who participated in the caper or for Christos, the ring leader. However, we were all in the same classroom that day, the day of the teacher's merciless humiliation!

The police had treated me humanely, but had my mother and my teacher?

There's an old saying that something good can emerge from any harmful or unpleasant situation. Life is not always fair, nor should it be. Fairness does not happen by itself, and unfairness is part of nature. Evidence abounds. Some trees, animals, and people are privileged, and some are not. Some are strong, some are weak, some are poor, and some are rich; some die young or are maimed, and some find themselves in war zones and are forced to flee. Why should I complain then about the damage some ill-informed people inflicted upon me during my passage through life? If nothing else, my mother's and teacher's paradigmatic treatment showed me *how not to be* and what not to do with my own children.

There's always something to be grateful for.

∞∞∞∞

The "authority" to discipline one's children doesn't always come with the requisite wisdom. Parents are responsible for raising their children but don't always know how. Societal norms often interfere with common sense. Enlightened societies have recognized all that and have taken appropriate steps to protect the young. Unfortunately, I grew up in a time and place where children had no rights. Despite it all, I recovered almost entirely.

Years later, it's fair to say I had brought some pride to the community as a couple of my books had seen the light of publication in the United States. My family, particularly my father, must have been too eager to spread the good news in the community. During one of my brief returns to the paternal hearth, while walking to the beach one day, I met that teacher who had shamed me in front of the entire class. He rushed over, put his arms around me as if I were his long-lost son, and kissed my cheeks and head with surprising affection. And then he did it once more as if for emphasis. There was no doubt he was thrilled to see me. I had not seen him for over two decades, but the community mill had worked in my favor. Some wanted to treat me to a drink or to be seen with me; one brought me some exquisite grapes from his vineyard.; another wanted to know if God existed. Whoever I met wanted to chat with me. An uncle borrowed from my father a publication about diaspora Greeks of Distinction in which I was included. He refused to return it, to my father's chagrin. I learned he would walk to the cafés in Patras with that book under his arm; he'd show my picture every chance he found, announcing proudly: "This is my nephew!" My modest achievements were unusual for my birthplace and had put my relatives and me on its map.

Despite the childhood flag caper, I was no longer a scorned member of the community. But the injuries remain.

Boquete, Panama
April 2024

The lyrics of a song from my youth came to mind as I lingered in bed for a few moments after waking up: "Mas ftanei mono ena kyma st'akroyiali," (All we need is a Wave by the Seashore), from a 1947 Greek hit. Other stanzas assure us that a small house by the shore would be enough for love to blossom in our hearts, in the hearts of a young couple in love. As the words rolled around in my mind, I couldn't decide if it was a love song or a lullaby.

I thought maybe my subconscious was creating an association with the small beach house I was considering buying and for which I had already made an offer. I reached for my mobile phone and quickly found the song -- thank you, YouTube! I recall it being a popular song growing up. Plus, the singer was one of our own, from our hometown. I listened to the old recording, and more thoughts rushed in.

It was in the early seventies. As a young professor at the University of North Carolina at Chapel Hill, I went to Chicago to read one of my research papers. A Greek-American colleague was also present; he was a University of Washington alumnus, like myself. We had worked together for a year on an intensive Bulgarian course. We met for dinner after the scholarly meeting at one of Chicago's hundreds of Greek restaurants.

Which restaurant we would go to was of no concern to me, except that we had agreed to go to a Greek restaurant as we both had Greek roots, and I had not eaten Greek food in a long while.

Those days, I lived in a cloud of anxiety ruled by my impatient ambitiousness. I had a young family, had recently gotten my doctorate, and was eager to show the world what I was made of. Only, I didn't know the answer myself. I merely existed at the time, not living or experiencing life as most people do - I was sweating it out for that far-off day of success and financial independence. And I was blindly driven.

Are most people confused? Or is it just the ambitious young people?

We took a taxi to Greektown. Once there, we started walking. I relied on my colleague to show the way, as Chicago was his hometown. So, I followed him, not paying much attention to the diverse character of this Greek part of Chicago, home to thousands of expatriate Hellenes.

The restaurant had many available seats, and my colleague chose a table near the center. We were served our order and were well into savoring our "keftedes" (meatballs) when we heard the tuning sound of stringed instruments.

Wonderful! We were going to have live music, I thought.

I glanced over my shoulder, and my gaze caught two guitarists preparing to play. I didn't think much of it and, appetizingly, plunged back into my "dolmathes" (stuffed peppers). Soon, guitar sounds started filling the restaurant ambiance. And then a singing voice: "Pote then onireftika na ziso makria apo tis patridas ta stena -- https://www.youtube.com/watch?v=LHE-rcsCu0c "(I never dreamt of living away from my country's narrow alleys.) I knew the song, even though I hadn't heard it since I left Greece nearly a dozen years prior. Its music and lyrics quickly resonated in my eager soul; its magic warmed my tortured heart. My throat felt cramped, and I felt transported far away. My mind airlifted me to my youth, then to my future, and back to reality.

Wait a minute!

That voice sounds so familiar; it's like a voice I had known very well; it's one of the singers I grew up with.

"That man sounds like a crooner I used to hear all the time," I told my Greek-American colleague.

"Mmhmm." He uttered condescendingly while pouring some retsina into our glasses. I returned to my ingesting reverie -- great taste on my taste buds, supreme contentment in my stomach, and a musical massage in my ears. A great mood was setting in.

"Aspres kordeles-- https://www.youtube.com/watch?v=fJfJtIMncTY " (White ribbons) -- another song soon began wafting past me. I slowed my chewing and caught myself humming along, then singing along. The mood was indeed improving.

"I could have sworn it was Maroudas," I said.

"It IS Maroudas!" he retorted, visibly annoyed. "That's why I brought you here, man!"

I really thought he was making fun of me. I looked at the bandstand again, closely examining the two people playing. I had never seen Maroudas and couldn't tell if my colleague was kidding. My logic came to my rescue or confusion: How could the great Maroudas be playing in a small Greek restaurant in Chicago? So, right there and then, I decided my colleague was certainly pulling my leg. Period. With a secret know-it-all smile, I went back to enjoying my plate.

The singing continued with "Meno se kapia geitonia -- https://www.youtube.com/watch?v=08Sdl-2-xGQ " (I live in some neighborhood). It was now staccatoing its way into my homesick soul. This was another song that Maroudas used to sing. I could swear it sounded just like what I remembered of Maroudas. My logic popped up again: some singers sound similar or imitate well. I turned to my worldly-behaving colleague with some doubts in my mind.

"Tell me, joking aside, don't you agree this man sounds like Maroudas?

"It is Maroudas, I tell you!!! How many times do I have to say it?"

Incredulous at my denseness and somewhat indignant, my colleague right then stomped his feet as if losing patience. He next waved our waiter over – it crossed my mind he'd pay and leave. Instead, he posed the question specifically for me to hear. The waiter confirmed that it was indeed Toni Maroudas. Pulling a folded newspaper page out of his back pocket, he showed us the small ad from the classifieds of a Chicago Greek newspaper. He added that one could also read about it on the sandwich board display at the front of the restaurant.

Confused me, I hadn't noticed it upon entering. Still in disbelief, I got up and went out to verify. A two-member band was displayed on a homemade sandwich board at the front of the restaurant: the renowned Tonis Maroudas was performing right here tonight! A tiny black-and-white picture of the singer with Sophia Loren was also affixed.

All doubts evaporated instantly, and I learned how acting like a certified fool feels.

A shockwave hit me; I felt great excitement and trepidation. This was a massive surprise for me. It was hard to believe: Maroudas playing in a small Chicago restaurant in just a two-man band?!

Maroudas must have been in his mid 50's at the time. He looked tired and life-weary. I had never seen pictures of him before but had heard his voice over the radio throughout my formative years. Awestruck and excited, I shyly approached him during a brief pause in his performance, composing myself as best I could. I told him I was also from Patras – I'm sure he was dying to know.

He was very receptive, and soon, during his break, he joined us at our table on his own initiative. We treated him to a drink. He hinted at a cigarette. Neither of us, two bookish young profs, smoked and couldn't oblige. He lit his own. We chatted for a while.

Looking at him, I tried to wrap my adulating mind around what was transpiring. This legend of a man, a demigod of contemporary Greek music, was now sitting next to me and at OUR very table! How could insignificant me merit to be graced with his exclusive presence?

I don't think the wine, my homesickness, or my love for his music could explain my mental state. Maroudas had produced several hit songs and appeared in a few movies; in 1957, he made a big splash by singing, "Tine afto pou to lene agapi? -- https://www.youtube.com/watch?v=MDMiUPcZst8 " (What do people call love?). This was a duet with the great Sophia Loren in "Boy on a Dolphin," a film from a bygone and innocent era. This man was a true living legend!

As we chatted, I struggled to reconcile my mind's giant projection of this man with the man before me. His music had provided abundant joy to an entire generation. Everyone knew his songs. He had brought boundless pride to Patras, my hometown; Zakynthos also claimed him. My great reverence for what he represented during my youth had made him a deity and placed him high on an inaccessible pedestal. And now this kind and gentle person, my hometown's musical colossus, lionized by thousands, sat at my table conversing with ME! Move over, Sophia Loren.

We talked about what we were doing, how long he was in the States, etc. There wasn't much else to talk about, certainly nothing of substance. It felt that our small talk was trivializing and wearing down the enchantment of the encounter.

It was apparent he had fallen on unpropitious times. The fact now was this great singer was currently working for peanuts in a nearly empty restaurant.

After a short while, he returned to the small stage and resumed singing.

Perhaps a humble cottage on a sandy beach is all we need.

Note: Tonis Maroudas passed away in 1988 from cancer; he was 68 years old and had only one lung when he died.

Rincon Beach, Panama
February 2022

A Message From Afar

Day One

I quickly skipped down the stairs from my eighth-floor beach condo. I was rushing to join Lena, my lady partner; she was waiting for me atop the hilly pine and eucalyptus forest. It's where we go for exercise and peace, our ritual ever since the high-season tourists flooded our otherwise tranquil resort. My pace grew faster while I tried to adjust my earphones – I listened to Richard Bach's seagull saga.

I had already reached the sidewalk when I heard a high-frequency noise that didn't belong to the story I was listening to. I caught the sound again, as it had now become louder. I turned my head to where the sound was coming from and walked back as the squeaking intensified. Something was crawling on the bushy side of the sidewalk. It was a greyish newborn kitten slithering like a snake toward me. Its eyes remained shut. Its umbilical cord, longer than its body, was trailing behind. There were no signs of its mother or any other cat. Its cries for help became louder as we approached each other. It was clear: this living thing, although blind, could not only hear but was eager for life; it was aware of my presence and was making its appeal to me, another living being.

I looked around for a piece of paper with which to grab it. I hardly deserve credit for thinking about what I was doing at that point -- it was some kind of an instinctive reaction. Picking up a plastic bag lying about, I wrapped it around the kitten; its body was large enough to fill just my hand, no more. As my thumb touched its head, I sensed its warmth and life. I marched resolutely back to the "portería," the doorkeeper's booth.

"¿Dónde está su madre?" (Where's its mother?), I asked. The man shrugged his shoulders, looking at me somewhat puzzled. Mind you, the people here are not unkind to animals. Stray dogs walk among the people and sleep anywhere on the sidewalks feeling completely confident and comfortable -- a civilized accommodation has resulted.

And here, at the gated community where we come to escape our northern hemisphere winters, a homeless cat community feeds on scraps from the workers' lunches, garbage dumpsters, and fields. These cats have grown to like us, as we have regularly fed them ourselves with better food bought at the farmers' market or in the town nearby. Interestingly, one of the cats the workers call Salomé has picked me out as her human. She never misses an opportunity to cozy up to me for a few minutes of caressing contact and cat talk. I feel genuinely graced and uplifted after each visit with her.

So, the attendant's puzzlement at seeing the newborn kitten in my hand was not what a northerner might have taken it to mean. With his head, he pointed to where the cats congregated. That was no less of a response than I had expected, and I hastened to deliver the kitten to its mother as was my plan. There were only two cats at the cat place at the time. Neither of them looked like the kitten's probable progenitor. No matter. I placed the kitten on the ground and resumed my walk. I was expected to reach the top of the forest in twenty-five minutes, and I was already running late -- my partner would be unhappy if I didn't show up on time.

A while later, just before dark, when Lena and I returned from our daily forest outing, I took her straight to where I had placed the kitten. It had managed to crawl off the plastic bag; it was now inside a concrete pavement corner blocking its way. The cold late evening had already started enveloping the place, and a much harder night was expected. It was a no-brainer that the kitten wouldn't survive the southern hemisphere night. Right away, while looking at me as if possessed by something urgent, my partner exclaimed:

"Мы заберем его домой" (We're taking him in), she said in her native Russian while stooping down to pick it up.

Of course, I had no objection, but I heard myself proclaim: "There will be some complications and some good feelings." My partner is used to my predictions, as this is my penchant. She ascribes it to my intuitive nature.

Once in the condo, ensuring the kitten's survival took precedence over our strict daily routine. My partner wasted no time creating a cozy home for the kitten: a shoebox with a bottle of warm water padded with a towel must have felt like nirvana after the cold outside. She started talking to it in tender tones and language that made me jealous. Such was a side of my partner I had not known -- the maternal instinct had seemingly taken over, was my first thought. The newborn became quiet, and I became silent, too. I suspected that my partner was secretly delighted. Indeed, the kitten's presence had brought some cherished warmth to our recent monotony. A ray of joy began springing in my heart. I have to confess: I like pets. And then again, it may be that I revere life.

Are we somehow wired for this sort of thing? I wondered.

An image from my childhood flashed through my mind:

"I'm about six or seven years old and lying in bed under covers. One recently born kitten is in my left armpit, another in my right armpit, a third between my legs, and a fourth in my hands on my tummy. I'm keeping them warm. I feel good. I remember I must have been doing this at night over a few days. A family authority figure gets a whiff of this and summarily yanks the kittens off me while scolding me angrily; then…. "

I never forgave her and will never forget it. I sobbed uncontrollably; it must have been a traumatic experience for me. It may well be why I've been striving to make it up to those flushed-down-the-toilet kittens ever since. Without further ado, I dedicate this story to them here and now.

Cruelty to animals is not a new thing. Humankind has practiced cruelty more often than one realizes. People can even be exceptionally cruel to each other. Let's face it: cruelty is part of our nature. Leaving institutionalized cruelty to animals aside, I believe there's a connection between people's station in life and animal cruelty. You can hardly expect, for example, starving people in a war-torn country to be kind to or even spare animals. Kindness to animals is not always a top priority. Undeniably, affluent societies offer good opportunities for animal life. Volunteers of all kinds devote a great deal of their time and resources to caring for animals. So, kindness to animals and cruelty must be part of human nature. It seems as if the design of our soul has good intentions unless the circumstances dictate otherwise. Sociologists might be interested in using this as a classificatory metric for the status of society's development. It won't surprise me if they have already done so.

"What shall we feed him?" I asked after a while, decisively taking the second seat in the rearing process and simultaneously compensating myself for my show of humanity by using an animate pronoun. In this context, the word for "it" and "him" is the same in Russian, and using "him" might have been my subconscious way of personifying the kitten.

"We can't feed it anything now; it won't open its mouth," she said. "What it needs is warmth and rest. Tomorrow, we'll go to town and get it a pacifier," she added, turning the lights in the kitten's bedroom off while gently pushing me out of the room.

I went out to our spacious balcony overlooking the oceanic vastness. Somewhere out there, about 8,000 miles into the endless west, was Australia; an enormous quantity of water, harboring an immense force, separated us. On calm days, long waves peacefully lap the beach as they've done tirelessly off and on for time immemorial. It occurred to me that the waves are not as docile on stormy days. They will pound the beach mercilessly, reshaping it for another day. And they always hold the nasty tsunami threat over our heads. Yeah, sometimes the ocean is kind, other times not so. Like people and how they treat animals was the idea.

I marveled at the cloudless sky with its starry chandelier hovering over the southern hemisphere. But the night chill quickly leaching into my bones abruptly dispensed with my musing, forcing me unapologetically back inside.

∞∞∞∞

Day Two

We sat down to breakfast, wishing our little guest would call us. I had already peeked at its box more than once. Betraying the first signs of attachment, Lena declared I should take the kitten to America. She had forgotten that we had agreed only to help it survive and return it to its "community" at our stay's end. I said nothing as the bonding process had also started taking root in me. The thought of appropriating the kitten and of life together had already occurred to me.

"How can you tell if it's a he or a she?" Lena asked. I was momentarily taken aback by this somewhat stupid question. If we wanted to show indifference to gender, this could be a good excuse for inattentiveness or ignorance.

"If you see two holes, it's a she; otherwise, it's a he," I blurted out in laconic precision, instantly regretting my rudeness. I had not paid attention either; what was important was to save the kitten, not to determine its gender membership, I thought.

No sooner had the kitten let out the first squeak than my partner rushed to its side. I followed closely behind. She picked it up tenderly and then went to the kitchen, where she had prepared an eyedropper bottle with store-bought cow's milk at room temperature. Every time the kitten would open its mouth to squeak, she'd try to drop some milk into it. But the kitten was too quick and unwilling to let any milk pass. We were both rather distraught, she more than I.

"We're going to lose him, I'm afraid," she lamented with a nascent tear in her eye. After trying a few more times, she gave up for the time being. She asked me to hold it while she refreshed the warm water bottle and refashioned its comfy box with a towel on top.

Neither of us had expected the effect or, rather -- permit me to put it less modestly -- the magic of my hands. It stopped whining as soon as it landed in my palm, and my fingers gently caressed it behind the ears. Indeed, I was now entering my expert cat mode. It clearly liked my treatment because its feet relaxed, and its breath evened. I began humming and enunciating my silly, home-spun feline sounds to up the ante. It was as if we were now in harmony, it and I.

Lena cast a relieved glance over at the twosome, deciding that now was a good time to get some food down. She put her thumb and index finger around its tiny mouth and gently forced the mouth open. Its white row of reddish gums came into view. She was able to release a drop or two. But the kitten ever so stubbornly turned its head away. Still, we both felt we were making good progress. A minute went by, and another drop got through. We decided it was good enough for the time being because the kitten went about it reluctantly. Lena picked it off my hand and gingerly placed it in its box. She covered it with a towel, leaving just a crack for air.

"It's a she," she suddenly whispered after we returned to our dinner. "It has two holes," she added. The empirical evidence had now emerged. We knew we had a female.

"Let's call her Gritis," she said after a considerable pause. She's grey like your Gris, she continued. Gris was my last cat, which fell victim to my globetrotting, but that's another story.

Our kitten now had a gender and a name; she was well on her way to forming a personality in our minds and hearts.

∞∞∞∞

Day Three

Unbeknownst to me, my partner had been getting up at night to refresh the hot water bottle and try to feed Gritis. Her efforts neither yielded great results nor encouraged greater hope, so she felt frustrated. The loss of sleep made her more discouraged and distressed. Lena asked me to hold Gritis in my usual "magical" manner in the morning. I was now the official house shaman -- if my hands couldn't do the trick, nothing could, was probably the operative understanding. A couple more drops of milk were allowed to pass Gritis' strict oral control before she went back to sleep. Lena refilled the warm water bottle and placed an extra warm water bottle outside next to her shoebox.

We went to town for our Saturday grocery shopping and to get a pacifier for Gritis' bottle as planned. However, when we got to the pharmacy, I realized I didn't know or couldn't remember the Spanish word for a pacifier. I decided to use an old tactic on the spur of the moment: mine my mental linguistic reservoir and resort to circumlocution. The closest I could come up with was the French word "biberon" for the pacifier.

"No sé como se dice en español, pero estoy buscando un biberón" (I don't know the word in Spanish, but I'm looking for a pacifier), I said in my usual above-the-fray demeanor. To my polyglot linguist's surprise and joy, the pharmacist immediately knew what I meant. He took me to the proper counter where a full array of exquisite and expensive pacifiers – "chupetes" -- was displayed.

It had been a long time since I had used my college French. I gleefully surmised the pharmacist must have known French until I discovered that the same word exists in Spanish. Words can cause lots of trouble, and languages constitute an incurable headache. Still, they can be a lot of fun and helpful at times.

We couldn't wait to return home to try the new Japanese pacifier. My caring partner had learned from her internet search that the sucking function was necessary for the kitten's feeding. We were now going to find out if it worked. She had also read that if the kitten does not exercise this function during the first six hours of its life, it never will. This first sucking imparts a lot of needed microbial cultures necessary to kick-start the kitten's immunity; moreover, one must observe strict hygienic conditions.

We rushed home with expectant excitement. Gritis was already calling us. I didn't want to admit it, but it seemed to me that her cries sounded a tad weaker. Although I said nothing, the impression hung ominously in my mind. I placed Gritis on my palm, her little head resting between my thumb and index finger. At the same time, my lady prepared a unique concoction culled from her internet search, presumably an adequate replacement for cat's milk. She gently picked Gritis off my hand and repeatedly tried to place a few drops into her mouth.

"She's taking it," Lena exclaimed in cheerful gratification. One drop got in, and then another, and yet another. We looked at each other in disbelief, feeling certain this was the turning point. We went as far as to high-five ourselves and felt confident we had already won the battle. Lena was thinking aloud; she would never let go of Gritis.

Deeper bonding was getting sealed.

∞∞∞∞

Day Four

The first thing I did upon getting up was to look after Gritis. I can't explain why, but I wanted to participate and did so every time Lena took her out of the box for feeding or cleaning. There was an attraction, a strong interest in her well-being, and joyful anticipation of good times. The kitten had now become our ward; she was in our care; we were going to help her manage her challenging first steps into our world. From her internet searches, Lena learned that, after feeding, gently massaging the lower part of the kitten's tummy causes urination. She thought that would be a perfect way to start getting Gritis potty-trained and help keep her sleeping area clean.

"What's this?" Lena asked, pointing to the dried-up umbilical cord still hanging from the kitten's navel.

This was a question I did not expect from a sophisticated person such as my lady, who happens to be a medical doctor. But it also occurred to me that I had failed to address that item myself earlier.

"Of course, you know what it is; it's her umbilical cord," I said, still wondering whether Lena had simply misfired in asking for the obvious.

"What shall we do with it?" she asked, placing Gritis in my hands. I was still incredulous that she would continue this play in absent-minded seriousness.

"Get me a pair of scissors," I said, looking at her from the corner of my eye in unconcealed disbelief. It was hard to believe we were having this conversation. Truth be told, Lena was not thinking about what she was saying. The concern for Gritis' well-being possessed her so much that her words bore no literal meaning. Instead, they were a shield from the fears consuming her mind. Lena was committed to the survival of this kitten. Spinning out of her semi-reverie, she uttered:

"She will be fine; she will grow slower and may not reach her ideal weight."

I was OK with that. The situation now seemed under control, but I didn't forget the importance of the first six-hour feeding. Contrarian words wanted to leap out of my mouth at that moment. Still, even though we didn't know whether that first necessary feeding had occurred, both of my females were doing fine. I decided to leave well enough alone.

∞∞∞∞

Day Five

My partner values her sleep so much that nothing can interfere with it. She's consistently dutiful about it. Yet, she's been getting up more than once every night to care for Gritis. She's done this, she explained, every time the kitten calls. Although we slept side by side, I had not heard anything despite being the lighter sleeper.

Lena's amazing caring may be understood as an unusual innate attraction for pets in some people. Pets fill a need: people need to trust but fear betrayal. The more disillusioned one is, and the more frequently one has been betrayed, the more likely one is to resort to pets. Pets seem to come with an iron-clad guarantee for unconditional friendship and non-betrayal. To your pet, it matters not whether you are rich or poor, young or old, male or female; it matters not whether you're overweight or slender, tall or short, beautiful or ugly. What matters is you, exclusively and categorically you. Your pet grants you permanent super-priority status; you are the veritable Número Uno. Your pet will never betray you.

Where can one find this premium quality of friendship?

When I came out of my mental rambling, the reality was waiting for me: Gritis refused to eat again. She stayed the course except for a few meager feedings of a recommended mixture.

"I think she's dying," Lena confessed, bursting into tears. She put her arms around me, her head leaning on my left shoulder while sobbing uncontrollably for what seemed to be a long while. My efforts to console her proved ineffective.

"I murdered her," she cried in histrionic exaggeration while snapping out of our embrace and stepping back. Her face was now assuming a dark expression. I was afraid she'd lapse into one of her mini-depression moods.

"What are you talking about? "I rushed to repair while quickly following up: "You've been doing everything possible." And I continued: "I don't know anyone who could have done more." Next, I enumerated the many things she had done, including sacrificing her very precious sleep. My efforts seemed to have only a minor momentary effect as the weeping resumed, albeit less intense. It appeared that she was intent on punishing herself. What was I to do? Should I let this follow its natural path and deal with the consequences, or should I continue with my helpful input?

The battle of rationality vs. emotionality was on.

If this was how Gritis' presence in our lives would end, I should reconsider my views on the meaning of pets. Pets, I've always maintained, enrich our lives; they reflect and complement our personalities to a large extent. How could such an innocent and harmless being bring harm? How could our best intentions and good actions lead to unintended pain?

I was forgetting that emotional attachment equals vulnerability.

∞∞∞∞

Day Six

I must be frank with you: things aren't going well. Lena has become quieter than usual. While I've placed myself on perpetual call for hand-healing sessions, Lena continues to clean Gritis daily. She does not miss an occasion to attempt to feed her. She never misses a call day or night. It's a side of hers that I hadn't seen before.

I am revising my assessment of her selfish traits.

She's clearly downcast and quite disheartened, as the kitten has now clamped her mouth shut. I am worried about what is coming next. The situation has affected me, and I am beginning to tiptoe around Lena and this entire state of affairs. We are now getting enveloped by a somber mood. We know we are losing ground, but do not want to give up.

The thought about the first critical feeding flashed again through my disquieted mind. And I decided to do something about it on my own. Without any specific plan in mind, I went downstairs. I aggressively marched up to the portería, where two attendants were chatting.

"¿Quién de ustedes ha estado echando a los gatitos?" (Who among you has been tossing out the kittens?), I heard myself interrogating. As if on cue, their mouths dropped open, looking at me incredulously and then quickly glancing at each other, wondering if I hadn't lost my marbles. They assured me no one ever dumps kittens out but that some cats themselves indeed do. Just the other day, one of them -- he had Gritis' mother in mind – discarded another one of her newborns there and pointed to where some big bushes were. He stopped me before I could rush over, explaining that nothing was there now. I did not have the heart to ask what had happened to Gritis' sibling. I figured they'd have told me if it was good news.

Sometimes, it's better not to know.

∞∞∞

Day Seven

We like to have breakfast on the east side; it feels good to let the gentle morning sun transition us to the new day. As I started eating my breakfast, Lena quietly entered the room and handed Gritis to me.

"Держи!" (hold her!); she said lifelessly, thinking that some "vital energy" from my hands would make Gritis feel better.

I held the kitten for a long time while humming a sweet but sad Greek tune about a loved one the trains had taken away. The song choice was entirely serendipitous -- earlier in the morning, I had caught its first couple of bars while shuffling through the files on my mp3. I continued holding Gritis, face away from the sun, so the weak morning sun would warm the small part my hands could not cover. This action seemed to relax her somewhat and to console me a bit, but our little friend, still refusing to eat, still with her eyes shut, was now lying motionless. And hope against hope, I remained still vested in believing she was merely resting and would be alright.

Oh, how blinding hope can be! It can lighten the present but cannot guarantee the future.

I heard Lena's prolonged, quiet weeping in the next room. She knew better and had now evidently given up for good. She returned to the breakfast room, where Gritis and I were, her eyes flooded with tears, feeling like an utter failure. She had something to confess, she managed to mumble. She pointed for me to sit down. Solemnly, she bent over the kitten's makeshift home, and with the utmost care, she picked her up. She then screwed up her eyes, fixed her grief-stricken gaze on mine, and hissed out: "Gritis is dying today!" Making a supreme effort to contain her sobbing, she added: "She'll be gone shortly." She then placed the kitten in my hands and made me promise to hold her till she was gone. "Focus on her pain!" she cautioned. "Ease off her pain! You can do it!".

I sensed that this entire episode may not have been accidental. Hardly anything comes our way fortuitously, but always with a message that gets lost if we are unprepared or unable to receive it, to figure it out. A torrent of thoughts rushed through my head. Involuntary comparisons bombarded my brain, questioning some long-held notions about life. I struggled to focus on the task and not let my mind wander away now. Bits of my humming resumed momentarily before the message took entirely over. My eyes glued on the kitten; I wondered if the energy flow had not reversed, no longer from me to Gritis, but the other way around. And in a split second, it all became clear, or so I thought: a powerful message had muscled its way through to me, and I had gotten it: *life is more precious than we think.*

I gently massaged Gritis' little legs; they were motionless. As if her mission were accomplished with the message delivered, she slightly moved her little head to indicate she was pleased, contented, and satisfied. I saw tangible signs of her letting out a deeper breath. Her tiny legs moved ever so slightly one more time.

And then, all of a sudden, she was no more.

∞∞∞∞

A while later, I made this entry in my journal:

"The kitten died about an hour ago after I held it for about 30 minutes, during which time I saw it relax and breathe out for the last time. Gritis' Seven Days of Passion came to an end today."

Lena cried a lot and is still mourning. She wanted to bury Gritis at the playground and "oratorio," the praying spot where she spends her mornings. I suggested finding a different place to forestall a daily, sad reminder for her. She agreed to let me bury it on the beach, which I did. It was an emotional experience for me, but I did it with great reverence in a way befitting a once-living being.

I couldn't hold back my tears. There's no doubt I'm sentimental; I've always been that. Above all, I was emotional for personal reasons: do you suppose we shower our pets with love because it hasn't been so with ourselves? Lena proved to be a soft soul as well. I was able to see another good side of hers. Gritis' coming to our lives was laden with meaning and significance. Her brief presence helped us discover and comprehend things about ourselves that we were either unaware of or had forgotten. There was every reason to be genuinely grateful to her, to a message-ridden, short-lived kitten named Gritis."

∞∞∞∞

Day Eleven

I set out to go to the forest where Lena was waiting for me. I decided to go by way of the beach. While passing by where I had buried Gritis only four days ago, I looked for the stick marking her grave. Seeing none, I approached. The sand burial mound I had formed lay demolished. A pit had taken its place; chewed-up pieces of the blue bag where I had placed the kitten lay scattered around. Her decaying flesh must have exuded enough of a smell through the bag and the pile of sand to attract some predatory animal, probably one of those hungry, errant dogs. And so, nothing was left of Gritis, and nothing was wasted: meaningful in life and beneficial in death.

Papudo, Chile
March 2012

The Two Thai Restaurants in Wailuku

M y waiter was about 35 years old, of average height, and well-built but with undeniable evidence of opulent nutrition. He had just served my order and was standing by my table.

"Haole call me Sam, but Thai name, Somsak, mean honor person." He began introducing himself in what seemed "unrepairable" accent and grammar. He looked at me before continuing as if scanning my face like a precision instrument: "I born and grow in Thailan and come to Maui seven years before. Like other, I come to America to make much money. In Seattle, open restauran, business good, make much money. Father wan me marry. He sen picture of Achara, Thai girl. Thai name mean beautiful angen."

Somsak punctuated every word as if it were an independent clause and shifted the stress toward the end of non-monosyllabic words. You could tell he had worked on his pronunciation somewhat but seemed to have run out of gas before moving on to higher parts of grammar.

I had certainly not asked him about himself. I was by now hungry and ready to dig in. He began his personal account as if that was part of my order. But it certainly wasn't. I had just finished a long afternoon meeting with a client in Wailuku and decided to have some dinner on the spur of the moment. My choice of restaurant was accidental -- Thai food aromata rammed my nostrils as I walked towards my car. As I like Thai food, the thought was, why not? I must have been hungry because I was already seated after violating one of my rules -- never eat at an empty restaurant. The idea, of course, is that a good restaurant is not ordinarily bare during peak hours.

"I love wife much, much," continued Somsak unabated.

Why was he telling me all this? I wanted to be left alone to enjoy my meal. I looked at him as I was preparing to figure out how to prevail without offending him. A simple glance at his pain-filled eyes held me back, however. I'm rather sensitive to people, you know. Most of the time, I can tell or think I can tell a lot about a person's inner world from a mere glimpse. I say "most of the time" out of false modesty because I don't want to irk those who might consider me presumptuous.

"But wife Achara cause many pain." Somsak went on. "Paren wan Achara to live with paren together in Maui. I come visit Maui one time. I much like islan, too. I think can make much money here, many touris need eat, good restauran. Firs, I not sure, strange feeling warn me not come, strange feeling tell me stay in Seattle. But wife Achara and wife paren say come, come, it be good. So, I sell restauran in Seattle, come to Wailuku; wife can be with paren together."

He paused to assess the situation before continuing his uninvited confessional. My mind, meanwhile, was assessing the damage Somsak was inflicting upon the English language. Since when had the singular number acquired exclusivity, and when was the past tense abolished?

"I open travel agency firs because no Thai restauran in Maui mean Maui no good for Thai restauran. Also, wife good travel agen, experience and speak English perfec. But soon big surprise: Thai restauran in Lahaina do good but location bad. I think Maui good for Thai restauran. We live in Wailuku, upstair from travel business. Wife paren live couple mile away house distric. Couple door from travel business Japanese restauran, still there now. Space between my travel agency and Japanese restauran become free, no time wase. I try to buy, but no sell. So I ren and open restauran here."

He paused again, shifting his weight onto the other foot while eagerly eyeing the front door. He had trouble with consonant clusters in final position; he skipped the "s" in "upstairs" and the "t" in "district," "waste," "agent," and "restaurant." He also tended to stress conjunctions and prepositions. His intonation was all over. Thai is a tonal language, meaning the same word can have different meanings depending on what is intended. Of course, I had no problem understanding him. My mind was automatically decoding his English to what is considered proper English.

"Firs, I open travel agency. Wife know business. Travel agency not cos too much to open. Restauran cos much to open: kitchen, counter, table, chair and other," he reasoned, looking at me meaningfully. "Better I stay in Seattle," he said after taking a deep breath and pressing his lips tightly together. "I hope enjoy meal tonigh," he interjected while holding onto his "podium" for dear life. Right there, as if an empathetic lightning hit me, I heard myself inviting him to sit by me, and in fact, without getting up, I pulled out a chair for him to join. Why did I do that? Hadn't I begun feeling annoyed at his impetuous initiative to force his private life on me?

Much of what I do when interacting with people is not by plan or the result of deep thought or any thinking. It's a spontaneous and highly rapid action instead that feels somewhat natural. This is how I do this sort of thing, and I can't recall a single time that it didn't turn out alright. My total take at that moment was: here's a suffering human being -- how would I like another human to have treated me if the shoe were on the other foot? As expected, Somsak accepted my invitation most gratefully and eagerly joined me at the table. It was as if we were now supposed to sit together, not as a guest and his server, but as two friends or associates.

"My wife paren very glad be with daughter," Somsak picked up where he had left off. "Because wife paren English no good, wife paren work in kitchen, make food like home and get money."

I visualized a happy family atmosphere with Thai spoken throughout -- the parents reunited with their beloved daughter and enjoying their growing grandchild. What could possibly be better? Yet, as I looked at his pained expression and felt his defeated demeanor, I wondered where Somsak was going with his story. Was there a sinister twist to it all? My curiosity took over, and I stopped eating or ate sporadically and absentmindedly. It's not unusual for my mind to interfere with that notorious "second brain." Most of the time, I consider food mere nutrition and no more. I hear myself saying strange things about it occasionally, like "I eat to live, not the other way around," or "If I'd had my druthers, I wouldn't eat at all -- I'd be a breatharian." Idle talk, to be sure.

Somsak continued his account relentlessly; he had goods to deliver, a load to unload, and a burden to lighten. He gave me to understand that his supposedly simple-minded in-laws proved as crafty as only Thais can be. They had managed to master the restaurant business within a few months and were enthralled with the daily cash count. But soon, they began feeling that the decent wages and the free meals Somsak was paying them to work alongside their daughter were not enough; they wanted more for themselves. Although he could understand that, why it had to be at his expense was unclear.

Wailuku was a small town of about ten thousand people at that time -- more than forty years ago. Besides several fast-food eateries, the city boasted decent restaurant food, including ethnic such as Japanese, Korean, Chinese, and Somsak's Thai.

This is a good spot for the reader to abandon reading further. Please, don't say I didn't warn you.

Without much fanfare, Somsak's in-laws left his employ and opened the second Thai restaurant around the corner from his. He told me indignantly that they used the money he had paid them -- the notorious Thai dowry for marrying their daughter. "Not to believe!" he uttered somewhat louder and full of grief and disappointment; another Thai restaurant to compete with him! They named it "Best Thai Food." He revealed that they even stole his mother's secret thin soy sauce recipe that had been kept in the family for generations. He could not forgive them. There wasn't enough business for either of them now, and his family life had been ruined. He loved Achara, and they used to enjoy being together. Now they can hardly stand to be in the same room; as of last week, she had moved in with her parents and had taken his only consolation, their child, with her.

He had sacrificed a successful Seattle restaurant business. He moved to Maui so they could be near their daughter and grandchild. The in-laws' ingratitude, greed, and lack of decency had been a severe blow to him. The poor fellow was suffocating right there in front of me. The injustice of it all was overwhelming, almost impossible to bear. His breathing accelerated; it was as if he was gasping for air. Above all, I sensed he wanted and needed validation from somebody; it didn't matter who. This is a most natural human need in similar circumstances. A psychologist would have been the one to do that had Somsak consulted with one. But an empathetic client would do just as well for now.

I had enough personal experience to size up the situation right away. One rarely needs to fear another person unless that other person is physically or emotionally close. In fact, the closer the other person is, as with relatives and beloveds, the greater the danger potential. Isn't that what family betrayal is all about?

Somsak looked at me, hankering for sympathy. He told me Achara was lovely. He had fallen in love with her the first time he saw the pictures some relatives had sent. She was about 23 then. He was about 30. He couldn't wait to travel back to Thailand to meet her. I imagined how meeting her in person had solidified his love. Her beautiful dark eyes must have pierced him with a strange welcoming power, telegraphing readiness to please, and lodging a massive hook in his heart. In my mind's eye, I saw him wrapping his hands around her sexy waist with uncontrollable glee, planting a passionate kiss on her inviting lips, and agreeing to marry her right away.

Misery knows no bounds and does not discriminate; it's like flooding water, filling every void with merciless horizontality. Somsak's entire life had been upended utterly through no fault of his own. Heaving emotions were inundating his soul. He felt profoundly wronged, lonely, desperate, and dejected, drowning in the incomprehensible injustice that had befallen him. It was like he was in a deep ocean, helpless and drowning. He searched his soul, seeking some kind of justification for all of this. He had been a good husband, a respectful and accommodating son-in-law, and as good a father as any loving parent. Overnight, his loved ones and his family had turned into his enemies. How is that possible? Why do people often betray their loved ones for money, and why are family bonds so fragile?

Greed. Greed. Greed.

I felt swelling anger in my heart. And who was to blame? Was it helpless Achara who sided with her parents by betraying her husband for fear of crossing them? I sensed her plight: torn between two raging opponents, her adoring husband, and her loving parents, she couldn't win. She was on the horns of a fatal dilemma that would turn her into a victim and an unwilling victimizer no matter which way she went. Oh, how she must have wished it could all go away! In my mind's eye, I saw her pleading with her parents to no avail. I pictured her sobbing uncontrollably, lying beside her husband, hoping for a miracle. She must have felt lost and was indeed lost. Their toddler couldn't have fared much better. Sensing the misery, I visualized her frequently crying at night and contributing to the mushrooming malaise.

Non-stop discord between the couple reigned supreme. Somsak blamed the in-laws. Achara was confused; she just wished it weren't so. She didn't know who to blame. Sadly, where emotion abounds, intellect atrophies. Undoubtedly, the blame falls squarely on the in-laws, the older people who should have known better. They should have had enough sense and wisdom to avoid such a predictable family calamity. Had prolonged poverty in their homeland cauterized their humanity?

With every passing day, sleeping became more challenging. When he managed to catch a couple of hours one night, Somsak dreamed he was alone in a bottomless pit that appeared cavernous and dimly lit. Achara and her parents stood around the pit's rim, looking down at him. Unable to climb out of the deep hole on his own after several attempts, he raised his arms, imploring them for help. Only their puzzled little girl, restrained by her mother, moved as if to lend a hand. They kept a frozen gaze on him, cold and cruel, and remained utterly motionless. His profound disappointment choked him; he collapsed to his knees, wailing. He woke up sobbing.

Poor Somsak poured his pain out. As for me, I had come to enjoy a Thai meal, in no way counting on all this undesirable emotional garniture. But the man was in a world of hurt. He had fallen into an unfathomable abyss through no fault of his own. He had endeavored to do everything right, as any decent person would have; his reward was absent, and a deadly stranglehold was suffocating him. I felt his unbearable pain to my core. Without thinking, I stopped eating and was switched to commiserating mode. My empathy reservoir emptied itself; I uttered what must have sounded like comforting platitudes, knowing how useless it was. It was like applying a penny-sized patch on a gushing, fist-sized hemorrhaging injury. Although this whole affair was none of my business, rage filled my mind; I felt like walking over to the "Best Thai Food" restaurant to have a few words with the old monsters who caused this desolation.

All the while, despairing, Somsak kept looking at the front door in vain, hoping for more customers. No one came. I was the only customer. An involuntary thought occurred to me: just how fresh was the food I'd been eating? It stands to reason that failing restaurants do not throw away unsold, already prepared dishes but put them back into the fridge for another day. Right away, I chided myself for such a trivial concern at such a moment.

Yeah, I felt sorry for him and somewhat for me, too. I was paying for and had the right to expect a healthful meal. But the reality of the man's tale quickly yanked me back to his suffering. Another thought popped into my head: the world has much sorrow, and it feels right to comfort the suffering, yet I had gone to a restaurant to enjoy a good meal. Would I want to come back? It's conceivable that the same line of thinking occurred with other customers subjected to Somsak's pained account. And they wouldn't come back. Would you?

Somsak was so wrapped up in his tale of woe that he didn't notice I had stopped eating, but in the end, he did.

"You not eat Tom Yum Goong," he said, pointing to my spicy shrimp soup bowl. Not feeling much appetite by then, I picked up my spoon and stopped mid-air. My appetite was completely gone. I lowered the spoon slowly and instinctively thought it was time to go.

"This is great food, but I don't feel hungry anymore." I heard myself saying. "Please take no offense. It's getting late. Do you mind fetching the bill?"

"Oh, no!" He responded emphatically. "Tonight meal on me." I tried to insist, but it was in vain.

I took my leave, shaking hands with him while dropping a twenty-dollar bill on the table. He tried to hand it back while I held my hands high, refusing to accept it. Then he stuffed it in my pocket with unmistakable finality. What was I to do? It was a tough choice between insult and embarrassment. Knowing he could not afford it, how could I accept such a heartfelt offering? Life is full of small and large conflicts. One has to make a choice. I let the bill stay in my pocket and left the restaurant in deep thought.

What would I have done if I were in Somsak's shoes? How could this festering sore be healed?

I walked out of Somsak's restaurant deep in thought, keeping my head low as is my wont when thinking, not paying much attention to where I was going. I must have passed a few storefronts or structures before my attention was drawn to a brighter light. My audible range was invaded by cheerful talk, which one hears after the third or fourth drink, accompanied by distorted speech and mindless humor. I looked instinctively over where the sound was coming from out of idle interest. Before me lay an average-size restaurant -- a few tables were occupied. I saw a good-looking young lady with a small child at her side standing by the hostess' podium. I looked up at the front of the restaurant: a lit sign read "Best Thai Food." My slow walk came to a stop; I retraced the few steps past the front door and entered. The atmosphere was definitely inviting. The young female figure approached me without delay, the little toddler trailing behind.

Don't we sometimes act without thinking? No one plans every step of their day; most of the time, we have an incomplete list of what we want to do while our daily drifting takes over. Our regular chores take up some of our time; they leave us with the impression that we're productive and have moved our day further. I don't know about you, but being goal-oriented, I find myself at the mercy of my planned schedule. I feel good if I'm advancing, accomplishing, and moving forward. I have no idea how you spend your day, and I don't know that I should care. As for this one of my moments, feeling like a zombie, I followed the hostess' lead to a table.

"Will this do, sir?" she asked in slightly accented but correct English. I nodded the same way when I agree to something I don't quite understand, am unsure about, or if it doesn't matter.

Politely, she placed the menu on the table and withdrew. I immediately noticed the menu was identical to Somsak's menu except for the background color. What was I doing here? Hadn't I just eaten? What's more, hadn't I just declined to finish my Thai meal? No, I was not hoping for another free meal; I was more in a fog than hungry. I was still trying to sort my thoughts after Somsak's story. Wait a minute! Didn't I just read "Best Thai Food?" out front? Of course!

This is the in-law's restaurant, dummy.

I wouldn't think much about such things, but having heard Somsak's story and now looking at the identical menu, something felt very wrong. Did his in-laws have no decency? Nothing at all?

An onerous foreboding began descending upon my soul.

Decent people find it hard to believe that someone from their close circle might cause significant harm one day. Yet, greed-guided thievery does not discriminate and knows no limits; the criminal mind begins to operate where the decent mind stops. But would you say that Somsak's in-laws are criminals? They certainly wouldn't think of themselves as such. Although what they did was wrong, it was not unlawful or prohibited but felt one hundred percent improper. Ultimately, it doesn't really matter what you and I think. We have a real victim and a perpetrator, and justice is called for. How can justice prevail here? Should the in-laws be required to shut down their restaurant and indemnify their son-in-law?

What about Somsak's wife? Isn't she a victim, too? What would you do in her shoes? Do you choose between your parents and your husband, the father of your child? What can you do to reconcile your family members? Why on earth do families often seem to develop serious conflicts? One is supposed to love or at least feel affection for one's family members, right? How can we explain today's beloved relatives frequently becoming tomorrow's mortal enemies? One day, you're ready to lay your life down for your wife or children; another day, you get tossed out and trampled with hatred as if you were the worst enemies or the least worthy human.

People's feelings cannot be trusted. In fact, your field of today's close ones provides the soil for the growth of tomorrow's enemies. If you ever experience this in its totality, can you ever bring yourself to love and trust anyone again? Doesn't your humanity suffer an irreversible loss?

Poor Somsak became a victim when he fell in love with beautiful Achara. Her own emotional attachments became the minefield in which Somsak got enmeshed. He didn't choose his in-laws; he only fell for Achara. Life is like that; don't tell me luck has nothing to do with it. On the contrary, you don't choose whom you fall in love with, just as you don't get to choose your own parents.

Luck. Luck. Luck.

As soon as I realized where I was, I hurriedly took a few dollar bills out of my wallet, placed them on the menu, and rushed out the front door. I didn't belong there. Besides, I was not hungry; my mind was burdened and burning with Somsak's story, and a lot of work awaited me at home. His account had seeped into my being, and the anger I had felt earlier had not dissipated; instead, it had beclouded my mind. I made it to my car and reached my Kihei condo about thirty minutes later, remembering nothing of the trip.

A few days passed, and other matters took precedence in my life. Somsak's narrative was still with me, simmering somewhere in my mind, until I went to the Safeway store that afternoon. The newspaper containers were stacked with the day's papers for sale by the entry. My eyes were assaulted by a Maui News headline: "Wailuku Restaurant Murder-Suicide?" Trembling and in great haste, I dropped two quarters into the slot and retrieved my copy – somebody pushed me gently aside as I was blocking the newspaper stand. I read: "Wailuku restauranteurs found dead in the early morning yesterday. A city disposal truck driver noticed a lifeless body in front of "Best Thai Food," a local establishment. The victim's clutching hands were firmly locked around a seven-inch chef's knife plunged deep into his chest. A second lifeless body was discovered in the restaurant's kitchen."

Pullman, Washington
September 2022

THE SNAKE ENCHANTER

Part I: Saturday, June 21, 2014.
Post Falls State Park, Washington.

I spent the night here in my camper without access to camping hookups. As you may be aware, this is not a problem when a motorhome is outfitted with all the necessities, such as a power generator, heater, and home comforts, like my Mercedes Sprinter Free Spirit. It's a lovely day now. Not a single cloud anywhere, and the temperature is perfect for me: 69 degrees. The steady western wind is to my liking; I can hear the gentle flapping of the festive park flags in the distance.

I'm alone in the park's motorhome section. A few picnic tables, partly under the shade, stand a few yards away. Small animals of varying sizes, like yellow pine chipmunks, yellow-bellied marmots, and squirrels, scurry just outside. A few American goldfinches, with their stunning black and yellow plumage, dart from branch to branch or land on the ground in search of food. The desire to pet one of them invades my heart; they're adorable. Black-capped chickadees donning their modest attire can be seen on their hopping rounds. At the same time, some of the ubiquitous American crows have greedily congregated around the dumpster -- I have no wish to be near them. The birds' chirps, whistles, trills, and croaks announce unstoppable life all around.

I feel swathed in the outdoors. I love this healthful peace and isolation and wonder why some people who have a choice prefer crowded cities with their congestion and pollution.

Nonetheless, I feel urged to delight you with a remarkable incident. I can't wait to share an extraordinary experience that just happened to me. I'm sure you will find it hard to believe.

While sitting on a nearby bench and playing a classical guitar piece, a 4–5-foot snake began crawling toward me. I decided I had better get out of there right away. However, my getting up frightened the serpent, and it quickly slinked away. So, I thought it was now safe to sit down anew and resume playing. No sooner had I started doing so than it appeared out of the bushes again and began its serpentine locomotion *toward me*. You don't suppose there's a musical connection? I wondered as I continued playing, and it kept slithering closer.

It occurred to me that, like the enchanted snakes of India, this reptile liked music, perhaps my kind of music in particular (do you suppose?) I was determined to find out -- was I turning into a snake charmer? I had been playing *Recuerdos de la Alhambra* by Francisco Tárrega, a Spanish guitarist and composer.

It seemed safer to climb on top of the park picnic table. I did so and returned to playing. With its lower jaw scraping the ground, the snake kept its head directed toward me; it then raised its upper jaw while its pitch-black tongue jutted in and out at the rhythm of my playing. I considered the possibility it might be a momentary coincidence, but this continued on and on. I dared a brief pause, and the tongue-lashing seemed to slacken. And just then, feeling uncomfortable with a serpent so close to me, I got up to leave. The snake promptly lowered its upper jaw, and the tongue vanished as the mouth got shut. It looked like it was putting its head down to express disappointment or something worse. Changing my mind for good measure, I resumed playing. Holding its upper jaw open again, the snake crept even closer.

I was now sitting tailor-fashion on the picnic table playing. At the same time, the snake, just a couple of feet below me on the ground, kept its gaze on me, its tongue hammering the air to the rhythm of my music! Or so I thought.

Was I locked into a Shahrazad scenario now: to continue playing for survival or risk getting fatally bitten if I attempted to walk off? The choice was obvious:

Da capo, back to the beginning, maestro!

My performance seemed to be called into encore service by categorical snake acclamation.

I sensed this to be a genuinely magical moment. Had I gotten into close communion with one of nature's wild beasts? Although I have an innate fear and dislike of snakes, this time, I felt as if I had made friends with one of them; a thin slice of my primordial fear of reptiles was discarded. Slowly, my uninvited guest crept under the park table, almost directly beneath me, and lay there, presumably listening to my music, until a pair of campers' footsteps startled it away. Alas!

I was in awe, and I had difficulty controlling my exhilaration. I felt disbelief. Had my senses deceived me? I couldn't wait to put every detail down in my diary. Just as I had finished writing it, a ranger, a wholesome-looking young lady, came by to collect the fees for my stay's pass. Before I paid her, unable to control my excitement, I asked her to stand by as I had something unbelievable to share with her that had just occurred! I read her my freshly written diary entry, but her lack of enthusiasm left me wondering if she thought I was nuts.

∞∞∞∞

I remained dumbfounded. There was plenty of evidence to exclude mere coincidence in this incident. I felt compelled to look into this to elucidate my ignorance about snakes, particularly how they perceive sounds. Reading that they have no ears and therefore couldn't hear was a non-starter. I knew they could perceive because I had witnessed their hearing. Let's not forget how eager I was to believe they could hear to validate the quality of my guitar playing — after all, a snake fan is better than no fan at all, right?

Snakes can hear, alright. It turns out they sense vibrations with their jaws. Humans perceive sounds through sound pressure, whereas snakes rely on sound-induced vibrations. A vestigial hearing organ is linked to the jaw bone inside a snake's head, which transmits the sound signal to the brain for interpretation.

You'll agree that hearing music is one thing, but reacting to it is something else. My snake's in-and-out rhythmical, piston-like tongue movements during my guitar playing cry out for an explanation. Is this a form of rhythm tapping, an expression of pleasure at the perceived sound akin to what humans perceive? I couldn't say. However, other animals have been reported to bob their heads with the beat.

Wait a minute! The serpent's energetic tongue thrashing may not relate to the rhythm. Instead, it may have everything to do with *Recuerdos de la Alhambra*, a musical composition distinguished for its reliance on *tremolo*. This is a guitar-playing technique involving two or three right-hand fingers, excluding the thumb, and alternately plucking the same string to produce a wavering effect of a musical note. However, responding to rhythm requires a higher ability, I believe. Some day, we shall know.

Be all that as it may, I had undeniably shared a magical moment with another species, a reptile, one of nature's wilder beasts. I was utterly dismayed, wanting to trust my senses but battling it out with my logic.

Part II: Saturday, August 16, 2014.
Lewis and Clark Trail State Park, Washington.

As we look at specific details of our lives, they may appear as staged by some omniscient power or as mere coincidences.

It has been a great day, with temperatures hovering around 80 degrees. I drove here a few hours ago. A sign indicating the park was full rippled through my equanimity as I entered the park's gate. Where was I to spend the night?

Although I occasionally succumb, I dislike planning my leisure time in advance. I prefer to get into my Free Spirit and set off for wherever the eyes glimpse, as the Russian saying goes. Despite the initial shock, I drove in, hoping for a cancellation in the meantime, or at the very least, to get a look at the campground for future reference. I spotted a uniformed worker riding a Cushman a bit further. He informed me that the common area for overnight camping was indeed filled but offered me a choice: leave or use the overflow area across the highway -- 12 bucks for overnight use.

Glancing at the desolate landscape in the direction he pointed, I blurted out,

"Does it have trees?" He assured me it did, and I opted to take a look. He officiously signaled for me to turn around and follow. He drove in front of me, and I followed close behind. Our twosome convoy leisurely crossed the railroad tracks and the highway. It proceeded equally unhurriedly onto a grove further away on the other side of the big road. Cushmans can go faster, but somebody's extent of authority must have insisted on 4 miles per hour.

While slowing down his workhorse even more, my guide pointed rather ceremoniously right and left where overnight camping spots were available. At this point, it didn't matter which site I picked or if I stayed there, except the place was empty, which was very much to my liking.

"There's one more area a bit further," he shouted. And off we drove once again. I picked the last spot in the second area without much ado and parked my Free Spirit.

I had been driving for a couple of hours, and it was about 3:30, my approximate siesta time. I can skip siestas and often do, but I become more productive and clear-headed if I don't. Without wasting much time, I hit the switch to extend the motor vehicle slide-out and did likewise with the built-in sofa bed. I even remembered to open the windows and the skylights. I flung the sizable side door open and shut its big screen door. Plentiful country air rushed in. The partially clouded sky framed by several giant trees on either side was now my picture window. An ample, bald hillside was crowning the distance past some old farm structures. I was suddenly plunged into a rustic environment; the sensation submerged me. I liked that. I dove into the sofa bed, locking the ambient landscape in my mind. I covered my eyes and went promptly to sleep.

After a restful nap, I grabbed my guitar and went to the picnic bench beside my vehicle. I started playing *Recuerdos de la Alhambra,* my favorite piece. No sooner had I gotten through about a third of the music than I perceived someone off to my right from the corner of my eye. A female ranger was standing about 70 yards away from me.

"A snake!" she yelled, pointing in front of her.

She was coming to make sure I had a Day Pass.

"I have one," I said, anticipating her query.

"I remember you," she said.

"I remember you too," I echoed back after a brief pause for recognition. "You sold me a pass at the Post Falls State Park a few months ago. What are you doing here?" I asked.

"I work at both places," she explained proudly.

"A snake *once again*," I said, returning to the point of interest and pointing at the spot where she had noticed today's snake.

"Yes, I remember your snake story," she said. Indeed, she was the first person I had read that account to.

"It was a big hit," I told her in jest but earnestly wishing it were so. "Isn't it funny?" I said. "We meet again a couple of months later, away from where we met the last time, and a snake seems to be our link in both places. Like Adam and Eve." She nodded pleasantly in polite agreement. "What kind of a snake was it?" I feigned genuine interest in prolonging the conversation and augmenting my knowledge.

"Garden snake," she said matter-of-factly, "like the last one, as I recall from what you told me." She explained that if a snake's tail is blunt, not pointed, it's a rattlesnake; otherwise, it's a harmless garden snake, especially if its color is solid green. My snakes were garden snakes; thank my lucky stars!

Her wholesome country figure cut a sharp silhouette against the late afternoon sky.

"Have a good night," she uttered professionally, taking her leave rather abruptly. My peripatetic mind was left to wonder why my guitar virtuosity could charm snakes but leave bucolic beauties unenchanted.

I strapped the guitar on my shoulder and began pacing toward where the last snake was sighted. I was strumming an 18th-century allegro. I was looking for that garden snake or any snake, whatever. The unshakable conviction had now taken hold that I was somehow empowered to bring snakes out in the open with the musical vibrations of my skillfully plucked guitar strings.

Boquete, Panama
November 2022

Ode To Life

Music from Dreams

I just fell out of bed, found out what key I had dreamed it in…, and played it." I heard Paul McCartney of the Beatles explain how he had composed "Yesterday," his big hit song.

He was then performing at the Obama White House in 2010. Though rare, receiving music in a dream has been known to occur whenever the inner divine chooses to favor us. We don't know the causes, circumstances, or reasons. It's a whim. A true gift was given to McCartney and, through him, to the rest of us for all time. It wasn't the direct result of hard work or even perspiration; it was more like inspiration, a process our mysterious world employs sparingly. It was divine magic! And it's not only with music -- precious gifts in other areas of knowledge can come from God knows where.

Let's assume that an unusual state of human consciousness exists that accepts some delivered item from the universe's warehouse – a passive process. This is to be distinguished from the state of consciousness that helps find solutions outside our standard patterns of thought, so often a blessing for problem-solving – an active process.

Have you ever been honored with a new melody in a dream? Chances are you …, but let me assume I know the answer and ask you another seemingly unrelated question: does your family have a family idol?

∞∞∞

Dyadya Vanya.

Some families are fortunate to have a family idol, a family member who serves as a beacon and guide to whom one goes for advice or money, whose tastes one wants to emulate, and whose approval one doesn't want to lose.

Dyadya Vanya (Uncle Vanya) was an idol for his extended family. More often than I would care to remember, Lana, my Belarusian companion, would bring up his name to serve as an example of decorum and family cohesion. Dyadya Vanya wouldn't do it this way; she would say à propos of anything: Dyadya Vanya would rinse his coffee cup; Dyadya Vanya would always take the garbage out; Dyadya Vanya would clean his wife's muddy boots; Dyadya Vanya would help his relatives, and so on. Over the years, I've had an earful of this and learned to disregard it. However, a sense of inadequacy would seep into my psyche – I felt inadequate compared to this most admirable uncle. The bar was simply set too high.

Although I never met Dyadya Vanya in person, other contacts occurred between us, once via Skype and several times by phone. Lana even planned for Dyadya Vanya and his wife to join us on holiday to the country of Georgia, where high government officials still received great benefits. During our Skype talk, I managed to irritate him by casually mentioning that some people consider Russia a dangerous neighbor, an aggressor nation. He invited me to visit him in Moscow to discuss matters further. I do regret not having taken advantage of these opportunities now. But maybe not.

∞∞∞∞

Clinton and Obama's Landcruiser.

Dyadya Vanya, who exactly was he? Without a doubt, a distinguished Russian apparatchik! A Belarusian by birth, he was a much-decorated Soviet and Russian Federation official, a Major General, and the General Director of organizations involved in developing and deploying strategic missile systems and repairing and maintaining aircraft, including spacecraft. He also tested rockets and space technology. He was, in fact, a high-ranking Russian official whom President Clinton entertained during an invited visit to the White House. And he was among those with whom Senators Obama and Lugar negotiated a nuclear treaty modification in 2005.

Lana also zealously proclaimed that Dyadya Vanya's official vehicle was the same Landcruiser that then-Senator Obama used during the 9-day US-Russia nuclear accord talks! This was difficult to believe, and I couldn't help but ask the General during a phone talk. Indeed, he confirmed the information. In fact, all three Landcruisers used by the nine-member US delegation during the negotiations were given over to their Russian counterparts! (Wasn't that a bribe, I wondered? And why not pick American cars for the American negotiators?)

Permit me, intelligent reader; let us instead focus on less mundane things now. I need to offer some notes directly from my journal for our story. They are about the events preceding Dyadya Vanya's death and apotheosis. They also introduce an "otherworldly" phenomenon that spawned over nearly three months and will be presented below.

∞∞∞∞

Diary entries
Dyadya Vanya is dying

August 1, 2015.

Dyadya Vanya, Lana's family idol, is dying of pancreatic cancer. He was given four months to live. As a doctor with a strong interest in nutrition, Lana has shown the family how to eat healthier foods for years, but almost no one has listened. I imagine Dyadya Vanya spent most of his life in opulent eating at banquets or at home, always following a culinary tradition with little nutritional validity. This could explain why, like so many others, he's succumbing to cancer – a tragic end to Dyadya Vanya's glorious life. And the same old thoughts run through my mind as I reflect on my own mortality: how unfortunate that life ends this way! One usually dies as one lives.

August 18, 2015.

Lana and her mother, Dyadya Vanya's only sibling, are currently visiting him in Moscow. He's in bad shape, she says, going in and out of consciousness with only one or two months to live and zero quality of life. Lana reports on their palatial Moscow home, which is surrounded by walls but luxurious on the inside.

August 21, 2015.

Lana called from her dying uncle's house, as planned. Except for the parents, the entire family had gathered in front of the computer to Skype with me: Dyadya Vanya's son Igor and his wife, and his son's wife, Anastasia and Lana. They were all eager to get to know me. They had questions, but I took the initiative to ask mine first. After a while, the ice was broken, as Lana later reported, and everything went swimmingly.

August 27, 2015.

Dyadya Vanya, the General Major, died today. He was 79 years old. Hundreds of people attended his funeral. The event was covered respectfully in the news media, print, and television; several publications highlighted his accomplishments and service to Mother Russia and lamented the significant loss. The country has undoubtedly lost a favorite son. And his family has lamentably lost their prized hero.

∞∞∞∞

Intriguing dream.

September 6, 2015.

I went back to sleep in the early morning hours and awoke with the following dream:

"I'm in a massive hall facing north. It's like a huge hangar. Except for a slightly raised platform at the front and towards the northeasternmost side of the hangar's area, where I see a small four-seater airplane, the floor is one level. There are three people on this plane. The captain is at the controls and ready; the co-pilot's seat is turned around. A man, who appears to be the lead singer, sits there facing backward but turns sideward, looking from behind the captain's seat to face the seated crowd. He starts singing a melody, and hundreds of people in the packed hall, all seated in what appear to be folding chairs, and those on the plane, begin to sing along. It's clearly a Russian minor key tune. I feel a strong desire to participate. A man, standing in front of me at the edge of the stage, slightly to my left and between the plane and me, who appears to be a pilot, is also humming along. He gets carried away at one point and joins in the singing louder. For a brief moment, our gazes lock, and he looks at me as if to apologize. I signal that everything is fine because his voice and singing are good. The song is long. At one point, I become aware of a large television screen high against the wall on my left, above, and to the plane's right. A pianist is shown accompanying the song. I notice he's seated in the far back of the hall, near the southwest corner. I'm moved by the somber-sweet melody everybody in the audience knows and is singing along with, smiling slightly. I'm not singing and can't make out the words, but I strongly feel it's a Russian song. I awaken." End of dream.

∞∞∞

I got up excited with the melody still playing in my head. I rushed to record the music and the dream. I was sure the tune existed and felt confident Lana, with her extensive repertoire of Russian songs, would recognize it. I got ahold of her and played the tune, but she had no idea. Acknowledging the melody's solemn sadness, she opined I may have foreseen some big catastrophe about to befall Russia. Without a doubt, far out. I was disappointed she didn't recognize the tune. I played the song in the exact key as I heard it and recorded it. It's in E minor.

I tried American and Russian song recognition software but could not identify the song. I was disheartened but not discouraged, and I vowed to keep looking.

At this time, I have no idea what the dream means or might mean. Is there a message there for me, for someone else? In searching for links from my recent personal life, I wonder if the appearance of a plane in the dream reflects my concerns about my own plane – has the time come to donate it and give up flying?

The dream image of me sitting amongst a crowd of seated participants in a vast hall thrusts itself into my awareness. They're all singing, but I'm not. They know the song, but I do not. Compared to my frequent isolation, I wonder if being in a crowd isn't a compensatory hint from the dream world.

It was a positive dream. The overall feeling is deep, sweet pain, with the tune leaving a compelling desire to learn it and participate in the singing.

September 12, 2015.

Dyadya Vanya was buried with full military honors, and his funeral was attended by an estimated "thousand" people, according to Lana. She sent me newspaper clippings and a lengthy biographical article about her uncle. He was a significant figure for Russia. This man had a glorious life in comparison to mine, I thought. Nonetheless, whether high and mighty or low and downtrodden, we all end up similarly.

Exit diary mode.

∞∞∞

Was the dream about Dyadya Vanya?

Days passed, and I still had no idea what the dream and its melody were about. At some point, a thought flashed through my mind, seemingly out of nowhere:

Could it be about Dyadya Vanya???

Given how moved my partner was by his death, I reasoned it was possible. He and I had spoken on Skype and the phone a few times, and I had grown to admire and respect him through Lana over the years. I listened to the dream's melody and enjoyed playing it on my guitar and blending it with the called-for chords. I indulged in its chord progression and relished and appreciated its becalming sweetness. I loved it! It felt just right. A divine melody, indeed.

Next, I returned to my dream notes and reread them carefully. I went back over, scrutinizing each and every detail again. I explored further, reminding myself that dreams are primarily about the dreamer. Alas, I couldn't find anything relating to my own current issues -- it had nothing to do with what I was involved with, i.e., there were no links. I was admittedly stymied.

Then again, perhaps it is a dream about the renowned uncle. What do you think?

∞∞∞∞

Re-enter diary mode:

September 14, 2015.

I was able to fire up Lana last night on my dream-received Russian melody. She started with her usual it's "simple melody" stuff. I cut her short -- this is what I got "from the universe," I burst out, pulling rank. A dream melody is different from ordinary dream material; at its core, it's solid, although it's subject to various interpretations; it's music and is consumable. It's a beautiful transmission from my dream, subconscious, or wherever. It's a wonderful melody, and in its character, it is Russian. I'm elated and feel great that something like this would choose me as the means of manifestation from the unknown to the known. I will not pretend to understand everything, for I clearly do not. However, I put my foot down on this: the melody is concrete.

Moreover, its simplicity does not mean it's unworthy of attention. I've understood that some of nature's simplest things work perfectly and are devoid of bells and whistles so often contributed by unclear thought. The tune can be played and listened to. As a matter of fact, Lana played and embellished it on the piano from my bare musical note transcription. And, as proof of my persuasive powers, she even wrote four verses for it in Russian relating to one's passing.

It occurred to me that exposing Dyadya Vanya's relatives to the dream and its melody might help alleviate some of the pain they're experiencing from losing their great family idol. And I have no doubt as to my role in this. I was handed a marvelous gift, and I might as well share it. In fact, I took it as a mission and now consider the balloon has been released.

September 28, 2015.

As I reread my dream of last Saturday, I'm in awe of its considerable detail. Lana finally talked to her mother about my dream with the "Russian" melody. I understood that it had landed well and that Lana had become a suitable transmitter by now. Her mother, she reports, had a lot of questions about my dream. She still has not mentioned it to her Moscow relatives, but it's a matter of time. Her mother will probably bring it up to her aunt, who will want more information.

October 16, 2015.

Dyadya Vanya appeared in several brief dream episodes and in a departing mode last night. In one, he was behind the wheel of a camper. He offered me a round sandwich containing a tasty mixture. I gave some to my son-in-law, who showed me some maggots wriggling out of it. In another episode, Dyadya Vanya was at the railway station tracks of my birthplace. I crossed some railroad tracks to meet him. I shook hands with him. His forearm felt like a bunch of asparagus. Other episodes, all about him, continued even after I had been interrupted to relieve myself. I understood them to confirm that my assigning the dream of September 9 to his death was probably correct.

∞∞∞∞∞

Skyping with Dyadya Vanya's family.
October 17, 2015.

Dyadya Vanya's family Skyped today as was arranged yesterday. They wanted to hear about my dream. I detailed it in my best Russian while they all listened patiently. Then Lana played the dream's melody on the piano. The family listened very carefully. Lana made her introduction about my "intuitive abilities," and, feeling like an anointed guru, I began telling them I had a vital conversation for them. They all listened carefully. I sensed they were hanging on each word. I explained to them that the purpose of the message and the melody was for them to use and hum it whenever they missed their departed one or needed to calm down and find serenity. This was like a gift from him to them and a kind of connection with him. I suggested they establish a ritual to get together and sing this melody to remember their deceased pater familias. Perhaps I was overplaying my hand here.

Lana played the tune on the piano well. However, she didn't feel that Tyeta Galya, the deceased General's widow, wanted or needed to talk. I felt otherwise. I had to press Lana to let her talk. The lady opened her heart with tears, telling how her husband was the best of men and about their wonderful life together. She thanked me profusely and asked me to help further.

Помогите! Help! She uttered, her chest heaving as she sobbed.

It was a significant emotional moment. I opined time was the best ally. Mourning, like other forms of grief, is a process. Such processes exist within us but are autonomous and usually subject to limited duration; they are part of life. One may affect their tempo. Still, in the end, they eventually go away on their own, converting themselves to a sad memory.

My mission is now accomplished. Right or wrong, I took it upon myself to put my dream's melody, a divine gift, to beneficial use. In this capacity, I served as an unambiguous conduit for "otherworldly" information transmission. I feel I did the right thing.

Exit diary mode.

∞∞∞∞

The melody.

I'm not a professional musician and did not seek access to a recording studio. I extracted what I thought were the most appropriate chords in this key. I tried my best to render the internal dynamics of the melody and bring out its undulating content, which, like long ocean waves, cradled me in their rhythmical and gentle stroking at some magical shore in a solemnly deliberate process.

I imagine a superb orchestra rendition someday with polyphonic elements and low-vibration instruments emulating what I felt during this remarkable dream. In a single-person performance, using Audacity, the well-known recording program, I combined in a simultaneous rendition seven separate tracks -- my amateur guitar solo and arpeggio accompaniment, as well as singing employing the five basic vowel sounds (a, e, i, o, u). At the end of this story, you will find the sound recording and the sheet music.

∞∞∞∞

Revisiting the dream seven years later.

As seven years have passed, Dyadya Vanya is no longer an occasional subject of conversation. Until the other day, my dream and its melody were lost in oblivion – they came back hauntingly while searching my sheet music file for some old song. My hand-written musical notation from my dream popped up. A strong feeling of unfinished business pervaded my being. Had I really understood that dream's message? As if guided by some force, I searched my diary for the dream. I compiled my relevant diary entries as they appear above. They span two-and-a-half months, from August 1, 2015, to October 17, 2015.

Had I really understood the dream's message? – the nagging question repeated itself. I reread the diary entries with an open mind and played the melody from my dream. It's not uncommon for dream interpretations to evolve over time as new insights emerge. My earlier assumption that the dream was about Dyadya Vanya, the Russian General, was based on Gestalt insight, a wholesale intuitive conceptualization affected by the event at the time. I felt the time was ripe for a more systematic approach and a radical revision.

With all the facts fresh in my mind, I posed the question most pointedly to my subconscious and promptly went to bed. From experience, I was hopeful that my overnight net would not turn up empty.

If you've never studied the world of dreams, be prepared to suspend judgment. An ever-expanding field of knowledge has claimed scientific status, beginning with Freud and Jung. For our purposes, dreams communicate with us through symbols that can be universal (archetypical) or personal. The correct interpretation of dream symbols in a given dream reveals a message for the dreamer. (A reader unfamiliar with dream analysis may have difficulty accepting some of the assumptions made here. As an inveterate skeptic myself, I see no harm in following the rest of the narrative for curiosity and enjoyment.)

I believe that a good indication of correct dream interpretation relies on the collective convergence of symbol understanding -- can a commonality be detected, and does the interpretation have a cohesive outcome? My melodious dream has several symbols.

∞∞∞∞

Parsing the dream.

• "I'm in a massive hall facing *north*." The main focus is "the northeasternmost side of the hangar's area, where I see a small four-seater airplane. Unlike my earlier understanding, this dream is not about Dyadya Vanya, my renowned Russian acquaintance. Nonetheless, it uses his death to highlight a primary concern of mine:

My acceptance of my own eventual death. Subsequent symbol analysis appears to confirm this conclusion.

• "There are three people on this parked plane. The captain is at the controls and ready" -- a big trip lies ahead; the plane is about to take off. My own big trip lies ahead,

my life will come to its inevitable end.

• "The co-pilot's seat is turned around." Small plane seats move fore and aft; some can go up and down, and their backs can even tilt forward and backward, but they never turn backward, so far as I know. In the dream, the co-pilot's unusual and counter-intuitive position calls attention to itself by challenging reality. Moreover, there's no other indication of contra-intuitive expectations in the rest of the dream; nothing unusual about a group of people sitting in a large hall or singing together. This is an excellent example of how dream symbols work.

The dream focuses our attention on the co-pilot; he's turned around as if looking at the place he's leaving behind. He's looking back at the life he's departing from. He's the lead singer and leads all in song. The melody sounds funereal but not lugubrious; the people singing it have serene expressions. The mood is solemn but tinged with contentment. All "sing along," i.e., all agree, as they accept the main message that

we all leave this life sooner or later.

• "A man, standing in front of me at the edge of the stage, slightly to my left and between the plane and me, who appears to be a pilot, is also humming along. He gets carried away at one point and joins in the singing louder. For a brief moment, our gazes lock, and he looks at me as if to apologize. I signal that everything is fine because his voice and singing are good." This is the dream's only direct and exclusive communication with the dreamer, me. The man is humming along, which means he agrees with everything because he understands the message. He sings louder, looking at me as if to ensure that I get the message and as if to apologize because that's how life is,

we all die.

• "The song is long." It plays throughout the dream. Its melody never stops,

its message endures for all time.

• "At one point, I become aware of a large television screen high against the wall on my left, above, and to the plane's right. A pianist is shown accompanying the song." Like an Irish wake, this nationwide day of a celebratory farewell marks the departure of a life, a natural consequence of our existence,

each living being's existence has a life and a death. Let's celebrate.

• "I'm moved by the somber-sweet melody everybody in the audience knows and is singing along with, smiling slightly." Everyone sang with a hint of a soft smile. The melody flows like a deep river, with no waves and no ripples; it's confidently triumphant and intensely profound. Its tonality is powerful but calm, as if to emphasize that everything is all right, as it should be.

It's life's lullaby.

The crowd singing in unison symbolizes they all accept the law of our existence,

life comes with a guaranteed death.

• "I'm not singing and can't make out the words." I'm different from the crowd and do not form part of its core because I still resist accepting the message about the inevitability of my own eventual demise.

Evidently, I have an immortality complex. When we sense or fear that we are approaching death's door, our soul softens, ushering in a shift away from the hardened, egotistical feel of "immortality." Life's end tames us; We want to be forgiven or assumed to have never sinned. We step into a mode of better behavior. We become more humane and less human if the latter is taken to mean a less hardened version of ourselves. I don't think I'm there yet.

My dream's melody, "Ode to Glory," was transmuted into "Ode to Life" as my belief evolved from referring to Dyadya Vanya's glorified death to the eternal glory that life represents. This dream focuses on a simple universal truth about life and death. Life without death is unthinkable; we all die – that's an undisputable law of nature, like it or not. Having difficulty accepting one's mortality is also natural. The occasion of Dyadya Vanya's passing triggered this dream due to my concerns and preoccupation with the whole meaning of life. Death was all around and close to me at the time; a lifelong friend had recently died, my brother was dying of prostate cancer, and Lana's father had a heart attack and was dying.

The dream's message is intended for the dreamer, me, after all!

Finally, while we may disagree about my suggested interpretations, my "Ode to Life" is authentic. Like McCartney's "Yesterday," you can hum, sing, play, and hear it.

∞∞∞∞

Notes

You can hear the Ode to Life melody on YouTube: https://youtu.be/4jC7VWNidBY. And here you have my best effort to capture the tune in musical notation:

Rincon Beach, Panama
December 2022

Appendix

ΕΦΉΜΕΡΗ ΦΉΜΗ

Καθώς ήμουν ξαπλωμένος στο κρεβάτι για λίγες στιγμές μετά το ξύπνημα, οι στίχοι ενός τραγουδιού από τα νιάτα μου με συνεπήραν: "Μας φτάνει μόνο ένα κύμα στ' ακρογιάλι", μια ελληνική επιτυχία του 1947. Οι λέξεις μας διαβεβαιώνουν ότι ένα μικρό σπίτι δίπλα στην ακρογιαλιά θα ήταν αρκετό για να ανθίσει ο έρωτας στις καρδιές μας, στις καρδιές ενός ερωτευμένου νεαρού ζευγαριού. Καθώς οι στίχοι στριφογύριζαν στο μυαλό μου, δεν μπορούσα να αποφασίσω αν ήταν ερωτικό τραγούδι ή νανούρισμα.

Σκέφτηκα ότι ίσως το υποσυνείδητό μου δημιουργούσε έναν συσχετισμό με το μικρό παραθαλάσσιο σπίτι που σκόπευα να αγοράσω και για το οποίο είχα ήδη κάνει προσφορά. Άρπαξα το κινητό μου και βρήκα γρήγορα το τραγούδι -- ευχαριστώ, YouTube! Θυμάμαι ότι ήταν ένα δημοφιλές τραγούδι όταν μεγάλωνα. Επιπλέον, ο τραγουδιστής ήταν δικός μας, από την πόλη μας. Άκουσα την παλιά ηχογράφηση και μου ήρθαν κι άλλες σκέψεις.

Ήταν στις αρχές της δεκαετίας του εβδομήντα. Ως νέος καθηγητής του Πανεπιστημίου της Βόρειας Καρολίνας στο Τσάπελ Χιλ, είχα πάει στο Σικάγο για να διαβάσω μια από τις ερευνητικές μου εργασίες. Ένας Ελληνοαμερικανός συνάδελφος βρισκόταν επίσης στο συνέδριο -- ήταν απόφοιτος του Πανεπιστημίου της Ουάσιγκτον όπως κι εγώ - είχαμε μοχθήσει έναν ολόκληρο χρόνο μαζί σε μια εντατική τάξη βουλγαρικής γλώσσας. Μετά την επιστημονική συνεδρίαση, συναντηθήκαμε για δείπνο σε ένα από τις εκατοντάδες των ελληνικών εστιατορίων του Σικάγο.

Το σε ποιο εστιατόριο θα πηγαίναμε δεν με απασχολούσε, μόνο που είχαμε συμφωνήσει να πάμε σε ένα ελληνικό εστιατόριο, καθώς είχαμε και οι δύο ελληνικές ρίζες, και μάλιστα εγώ είχα πολύ καιρό να φάω ελληνικό φαγητό.

Εκείνες τις μέρες ζούσα σε ένα σύννεφο άγχους που το κυβερνούσαν οι επίμονες φιλοδοξίες μου. Είχα μια νεαρή οικογένεια, είχα πάρει πρόσφατα το διδακτορικό μου, και ήμουν ανυπόμονος να δείξω στον κόσμο από τι ήμουν πλασμένος. Μόνο που δεν ήξερα ο ίδιος την απάντηση. Απλώς υπήρχα τότε, χωρίς να ζω ή να περνάω τη ζωή όπως οι περισσότεροι άνθρωποι - ιδροκοπούσα για εκείνη τη μακρινή μέρα της επιτυχίας και της οικονομικής ανεξαρτησίας. Και ήμουν τυφλά προσανατολισμένος.

Είναι οι περισσότεροι άνθρωποι συγχυσμένοι; Ή μήπως μόνο οι φιλόδοξοι νέοι;

Πιάσαμε ένα ταξί για την Greektown, τη μικρή Ελλάδα του Σικάγο. Μόλις φτάσαμε εκεί, προχωρήσαμε με τα πόδια. Βασίστηκα στον συνάδελφό μου να μας δείξει τον δρόμο, αφού ήταν από εκεί. Έτσι, τον ακολούθησα, χωρίς να δίνω ιδιαίτερη σημασία στον πολυποίκιλο χαρακτήρα αυτού του ελληνικού κομματιού της Αμερικής, που φιλοξενεί χιλιάδες ομογενείς Έλληνες.

Υπήρχαν πολλά διαθέσιμα καθίσματα στο εστιατόριο, και ο συνάδελφός μου διάλεξε ένα τραπέζι κοντά στο κέντρο. Μας σερβίρισαν την παραγγελία μας και είχαμε αρχίσει να απολαμβάνουμε τους κεφτέδες, όταν ακούσαμε τον κουρδιστό ήχο έγχορδων οργάνων..

Υπέροχα! Θα είχαμε και ζωντανή μουσική, κατάλαβα.

Έριξα μια ματιά πάνω από τον ώμο μου και το βλέμμα μου έπιασε δύο κιθαρίστες που ετοιμάζονταν να παίξουν. Δεν το σκέφτηκα και πολύ και, με όρεξη, βυθίστηκα ξανά στους ντολμάδες μου. Σύντομα οι ήχοι της κιθάρας άρχισαν να πλημμυρίζουν την ατμόσφαιρα του εστιατορίου. Και τότε μια φωνή άρχισε να τραγουδάει: "Ποτέ δεν ονειρεύτηκα να ζήσω μακριά από της πατρίδας τα στενά -- https://www.youtube.com/watch?v=LHE-rcsCu0c. " Ήξερα το τραγούδι βέβαια, αν και είχα να το ακούσω από τότε που είχα αφήσει την Ελλάδα σχεδόν δώδεκα χρόνια πριν. Η μουσική και οι στίχοι του γρήγορα αντήχησαν στην πρόθυμη ψυχή μου- η μαγικότητά του ζέστανε τη βασανισμένη καρδιά μου. Ο λαιμός μου ένιωσε να σφίγγεται και αισθάνθηκα να μεταφέρομαι μακριά. Το μυαλό μου με εκτίναξε στα νιάτα μου, έπειτα στο μέλλον μου, και με προσγείωσε πάλι στην πραγματικότητα.

Για μισό λεπτό! Αυτή η φωνή μου φαίνεται τόσο γνώριμη...

"Μοιάζει με έναν τραγουδιστή που άκουγα συχνά", είπα στον Ελληνοαμερικανό συνάδελφό μου, δείχνοντας το ερμηνευτή με ένα κίνημα κεφαλής, όπως μόνο οι Έλληνες το κάνουν. "Είναι μια πολύ γνωστή φωνή από τα νεανικά μου χρόνια," πρόσθεσα.

"Μμμμ!" Ξεστόμισε συγκαταβατικά ο φίλος μου ενώ έβαζε ρετσίνα στα ποτήρια μας. Επέστρεψα στην καταναλωτική μου ευδαιμονία -- υπέροχη αίσθηση στους γευστικούς μου κάλυκες, υπέρτατη ικανοποίηση στο στομάχι μου και ένα μουσικό μασάζ στα αυτιά μου. Μια υπέροχη διάθεση είχε αρχίσει να δημιουργείται.

Μετά από λίγο ένα άλλο κομμάτι εισέβαλε στο περιβάλλον -- "Άσπρες κορδέλες-- https://www.youtube.com/watch?v=fJfJtIMncTY "– κι' άρχισε σύντομα να με παρασέρνει. Επιβράδυνα το μάσημά μου και πιάστηκα να σιγοτραγουδάω και στη συνέχεια να τραγουδάω μαζί του. Η διάθεση πραγματικά καλυτέρευε.

"Θα ορκιζόμουν ότι είναι ο Μαρούδας", είπα.

"ΕΙΝΑΙ ο Μαρούδας!" ανταπάντησε ο συνάδελφος μου, φανερά ενοχλημένος. "Γι' αυτό σε έφερα εδώ, κύριε!"

Πραγματικά νόμιζα ότι με κορόιδευε. Κοίταξα ξανά την εξέδρα της μπάντας, εξετάζοντας προσεκτικά τους δύο ανθρώπους που έπαιζαν. Δεν είχα δει ποτέ τον Μαρούδα και δεν μπορούσα να καταλάβω αν ο συνάδελφός μου αστειευόταν. Η λογική μου ήρθε να με σώσει ή να με μπερδέψει: Πώς ήταν δυνατόν ο μεγάλος Μαρούδας να παίζει σε ένα μικρό ελληνικό εστιατόριο στο Σικάγο; Έτσι, εκείνη τη στιγμή, αποφάσισα ότι ο συνάδελφός μου σίγουρα με κορόιδευε. Τελεία και παύλα. Με ένα κρυφό χαμόγελο του ξερόλα, γύρισα να απολαύσω το πιάτο μου.

Το τραγούδισμα συνεχίστηκε. "Μένω σε κάποια γειτονιά-- https://www.youtube.com/watch?v=08Sdl-2-xGQ ", έμπαινε τώρα στακάτο στη νοσταλγική μου ψυχή. Αυτό ήταν ένα άλλο τραγούδι που τραγουδούσε ο Μαρούδας. Μπορούσα να ορκιστώ, ότι ακουγόταν εκατό τοις εκατό σαν αυτό που θυμόμουν από τον Μαρούδα, οπωσδήποτε. Η λογική μου πετάχτηκε πάλι: κάποιοι τραγουδιστές ακούγονται παρόμοιοι ή μιμούνται καλά. Απευθύνθηκα στον κοσμογυρισμένο συνάδελφό μου με λίγες αμφιβολίες στο μυαλό μου.

"Πες μου, αλήθεια, χωρίς πλάκα, δεν συμφωνείς ότι αυτός ο άνθρωπος τραγουδάει σαν τον Μαρούδα;"

"Είναι ο Μαρούδας, σου λέω!!! Πόσες φορές πρέπει να στο πω;"

Κατάπληκτος με την αμυαλοσύνη μου και κάπως αγανακτισμένος, ο συνάδελφός μου μόλις τότε χτύπησε τα πόδια του σαν να έχανε την υπομονή του. Στη συνέχεια έκανε νόημα στο σερβιτόρο μας να πλησιάσει - μου πέρασε από το μυαλό ότι θα πλήρωνε και θα έφευγε. Αντ' αυτού, έθεσε την ερώτηση ειδικά για να την ακούσω εγώ. Ο σερβιτόρος επιβεβαίωσε ότι επρόκειτο πράγματι για τον Τόνυ Μαρούδα - έβγαλε μάλιστα από την πίσω τσέπη του μια διπλωμένη σελίδα εφημερίδας και μας έδειξε τη μικρή αγγελία μιας ελληνικής εφημερίδας του Σικάγο. Πρόσθεσε ότι μπορούσε κανείς να διαβάσει γι' αυτό και στην ταμπέλα στην είσοδο του εστιατορίου.

Αφελής εγώ, δεν το είχα προσέξει κατά την είσοδό μου. Παρόλα αυτά, με δυσπιστία, σηκώθηκα και βγήκα έξω για να το ελέγξω σαν να επρόκειτο για επιστημονική ερεύνα. Ένα διμελές συγκρότημα παρουσιαζόταν σε ένα αυτοσχέδιο τρίποδο στην πρόσοψη του εστιατορίου: ο διάσημος Τώνης Μαρούδας εμφανιζόταν απόψε ακριβώς εδώ! Μια μικροσκοπική ασπρόμαυρη φωτογραφία του τραγουδιστή με τη Σοφία Λόρεν ήταν επίσης προσαρτημένη.

Όλες οι αμφιβολίες εξατμίστηκαν αμέσως και έμαθα πώς νιώθει ένας πιστοποιημένος ηλίθιος.

Ένα κύμα σοκ με χτύπησε- ένιωσα μεγάλο ενθουσιασμό και συγκίνηση. Αυτή ήταν μια τεράστια έκπληξη για μένα. Ήταν δύσκολο να το πιστέψω: Ο μεγάλος Μαρούδας να παίζει σε ένα μικρό εστιατόριο του Σικάγο σε μια μόνο διμελή μπάντα!

Ο Μαρούδας πρέπει να ήταν γύρω στα 50 εκείνη την εποχή. Φαινόταν ταλαιπωρημένος και κουρασμένος από τη ζωή. Δεν είχα δει φωτογραφίες του, αλλά είχα ακούσει τη φωνή του από το ραδιόφωνο σε όλη την παιδική μου ηλικία. Με δέος και ενθουσιασμό, τον πλησίασα ντροπαλά κατά τη διάρκεια μιας σύντομης παύσης στην παράστασή του και συγκρατούμενος όσο καλύτερα μπορούσα, κατάφερα να του πω ότι ήμουν και εγώ από την Πάτρα -- είμαι σίγουρος ότι λαχταρούσε να το μάθει.

Ήταν πολύ δεκτικός και μάλιστα σε λίγο, κατά τη διάρκεια του διαλείμματός του, ήρθε στο τραπέζι μας με δική του πρωτοβουλία. Τον κεράσαμε ένα ποτό. Μας πρότεινε ένα τσιγάρο. Κανένας από εμάς, δύο βιβλιοφάγοι νεαροί καθηγητές, δεν κάπνιζε και δεν μπορούσαμε να του κάνουμε τη χάρη. Άναψε το δικό του. Κουβεντιάσαμε για λίγο.

Καθώς τον κοίταζα, προσπάθησα να καταλάβω τι συνέβαινε στο μυαλό μου. Αυτός ο θρύλος ανθρώπου, ένας ημίθεος της σύγχρονης ελληνικής μουσικής, καθόταν τώρα δίπλα μου, στο δικό μας το τραπέζι! Πώς θα μπορούσα εγώ ο ασήμαντος να αξιωθώ να με τιμήσει τέτοιος άνθρωπος με την αποκλειστική του παρουσία;

Δεν νομίζω ότι το κρασί, η νοσταλγία μου για την πατρίδα ή η αγάπη μου για τη μουσική του θα μπορούσαν να εξηγήσουν την ψυχική μου κατάσταση. Ο Μαρούδας είχε κάνει αρκετές επιτυχίες και είχε επίσης εμφανιστεί σε μερικές ταινίες -- το 1957, έκανε μεγάλη εντύπωση με το "Τι είναι αυτό που το λένε αγάπη. -- https://www.youtube.com/watch?v=MDMiUPcZst8 " Ήταν ένα ντουέτο με τη μεγάλη Σοφία Λόρεν στο "Το παιδί και το δελφίνι", μια ταινία περασμένης και αθώας εποχής.

Καθώς κουβεντιάζαμε, πάλευα να συμβιβάσω τη γιγαντιαία προβολή του μυαλού μου γι' αυτόν τον άνθρωπο με το άτομο μπροστά μου. Η μουσική του είχε προσφέρει άφθονη χαρά σε μια ολόκληρη γενιά. Όλοι ήξεραν τα τραγούδια του. Είχε φέρει απεριόριστη υπερηφάνεια στην Πάτρα -- τον διεκδικούσε και η Ζάκυνθος. Ο μεγάλος σεβασμός που έτρεφα στα νιάτα μου για αυτό που εκπροσωπούσε αυτός, τον είχε κάνει θεότητα και τον είχε τοποθετήσει ψηλά σε ένα απρόσιτο βάθρο. Και τώρα αυτός ο ευγενικός και καλοκάγαθος άνθρωπος, ο μουσικός κολοσσός της γενέτειράς μου που αποθεώθηκε από χιλιάδες ανθρώπους, καθόταν στο τραπέζι μου και συνομιλούσε ΜΑΖΙ ΜΟΥ! Κάνε στην άκρη, Σοφία Λόρεν!

Μιλήσαμε για το τι κάναμε, για πόσο καιρό βρισκόταν στις ΗΠΑ και ούτω καθεξής. Δεν υπήρχαν πολλά άλλα να συζητήσουμε, σίγουρα τίποτα ουσιαστικό. Ένιωθα ότι η μικροσυζήτησή μας υποβάθμιζε και έφθειρε τη γοητεία της συνάντησης.

Ήταν προφανές ότι είχε καταπέσει σε δύσκολες στιγμές. Το γεγονός τώρα ήταν ότι αυτός ο μεγάλος τραγουδιστής δούλευε αυτή τη στιγμή για ψίχουλα σε ένα σχεδόν άδειο εστιατόριο.

Μετά από λίγο, χωρίς ιδιαίτερο ενθουσιασμό επέστρεψε στη μικρή εξέδρα και συνέχισε το τραγούδι.

Ίσως ένα ταπεινό σπιτάκι σε μια αμμουδιά είναι ακριβώς αυτό που χρειαζόμαστε!

Σημείωση: Ο Τώνης Μαρούδας απεβίωσε μόνο με έναν πνεύμονα το 1988 από καρκίνο. Ήταν 68 ετών.

Μποκέτε, Παναμάς
Φεβρουάριος 2022

Un mensaje de lejos

Dia uno

Salté rápidamente las escaleras descendiendo del octavo piso de mi condominio playero. Me apresuraba a juntarme con Lena, mi compañera, quien estaba esperando en lo alto del bosque de pinos y eucaliptos. Allí es donde solemos ir para ejercitarnos y encontrar paz. Esto se ha convertido en nuestro ritual desde que los turistas de temporada alta empezaron a inundar nuestro balneario, por lo demás muy tranquilo. Mientras caminaba enérgicamente, traté de ajustar mis audífonos -- estaba escuchando la saga de gaviotas de Richard Bach.

Ya había llegado a la acera cuando escuché un ruido de alta frecuencia que no parecía ser parte de la novela que estaba escuchando. Oí el sonido de nuevo, ya que ahora se había vuelto más fuerte. Volví la cabeza hacia donde provenía, y caminé hacia atrás mientras los chirridos se intensificaban. Algo se arrastraba por el lado elevado de la acera. Era un gatito grisáceo recién nacido deslizándose como una serpiente hacia mí. Sus ojos seguían cerrados. Su cordón umbilical, más largo que su cuerpo, se arrastraba detrás de él. No había signos de su madre o cualquier otro gato. Sus gritos de ayuda se hicieron más fuertes a medida que nos acercábamos, él y yo. Estaba claro: este ser vivo, aunque ciego, no solo podía oír, sino que estaba ansioso por la vida; era consciente de mi presencia y me hacía un llamamiento a mí, a otro ser vivo.

Busqué un pedazo de papel para agarrar al gatito. Casi no merezco el crédito por pensar en lo que estaba haciendo en ese momento -- fue como una especie de reacción instintiva. Recogiendo una bolsa de plástico que estaba tirada, la envolví alrededor del gatito; su cuerpo era lo suficientemente grande como para llenar solo mi mano, no más. Cuando mi pulgar tocó su cabeza, sentí su calor, sentí su vida. Resueltamente, volví a la "portería", la entrada a nuestro edificio de condominio.

"¿Dónde está su madre?" pregunté. El hombre se encogió de hombros mirándome algo desconcertado.

Eso sí, la gente aquí no es cruel con los animales. De hecho, los perros callejeros caminan entre la gente y duermen en cualquier lugar de las aceras sintiéndose completamente seguros y cómodos. Ha resultado un ajuste civilizado. Y aquí, en la comunidad cerrada donde vinimos a escapar de nuestros inviernos del hemisferio norte, hay una comunidad de gatos sin hogar que se alimenta de sobras de los almuerzos de los jardineros y de lo que puedan obtener de los basureros y los campos. A estos gatos les hemos llegado a gustar mucho, ya que nos hemos complacido en alimentarlos regularmente con mejores alimentos comprados en el mercado de agricultores o en la ciudad cercana. De hecho, una de las gatas quien los trabajadores llaman Salomé, me eligió como su ser humano y nunca pierde la oportunidad de acomodarse conmigo durante unos minutos de contacto y charlas de gato. Me siento verdaderamente agradecido y animado después de cada visita a Salomé.

∞∞∞∞

Por lo tanto, el desconcierto del portero al ver al gatito recién nacido en mi mano no era lo que un norteño podría haber considerado que significaba. Con su cabeza señaló hacia donde solían juntarse los gatos. Eso era casi la respuesta que esperaba, y me apresuré a entregarle el gatito a su madre como era mi plan. Sólo había dos gatos en el lugar de gatos en ese momento. Ninguno de ellos parecía ser el progenitor probable del gatito. No importaba. Coloqué al gatito en el suelo y reanudé mi caminata apresuradamente: Tenía que llegar a la cima del bosque en veinticinco minutos y ya estaba llegando tarde. Mi pareja se preocuparía si yo no apareciera a tiempo. Lo sabía con seguridad.

Un poco más tarde, justo antes de que oscureciera, cuando Lena y yo regresamos de nuestra excursión diaria al bosque, la llevé directamente a donde había colocado el gatito. El pobrecito estaba solo; había logrado arrastrarse fuera de la bolsa de plástico y meterse en una esquina interior formada por el pavimento de hormigón que ahora estaba bloqueando su camino. La tarde fría ya había comenzado a envolver el lugar, y la noche mucho más fría seguiría. Era obvio que el gatito no sobreviviría. De inmediato, mi compañera, mientras se veía como si estuviera poseída por algo verdaderamente urgente, exclamó:

"Мы заберем его домой (lo llevamos a casa)," dijo en su ruso natal mientras se agachaba para recogerlo.

Por supuesto, no tuve ninguna objeción, pero me oí a mí mismo proclamar: "Habrá algunas complicaciones, pero también buenos sentimientos". Mi pareja está acostumbrada a mis predicciones, ya que esta es una inclinación mía. Lo atribuye a mi naturaleza intuitiva.

Una vez en el condominio, asegurar la supervivencia del gatito tuvo prioridad sobre nuestra estricta rutina diaria. Mi compañera no perdió tiempo en crear un hogar acogedor para el gatito. Una caja de zapatos con una botella de agua tibia, acolchada con una toalla, debe haberse sentido como nirvana después del frío exterior. Ella comenzó a hablarle al gatito en un tono tan tierno y en un lenguaje que me puso celoso. Este era un lado de mi compañera que no conocía: el instinto de madre aparentemente se había hecho cargo -- fue mi primer pensamiento. El recién nacido se quedó en silencio; y también me quedé callado. Sospeché que mi pareja estaba secretamente encantada. De hecho, la presencia del gatito había traído un calor preciado a nuestra reciente monotonía, y un rayo de alegría comenzó a brotar de mi corazón. Tengo que confesar: me gustan las mascotas. Y, de nuevo, puede ser que reverencie la vida.

"¿Estamos programados de alguna manera para este tipo de cosas?" me pregunté.

Una imagen de mi niñez brilló a través de mi mente. Debo haber tenido unos seis o siete años. Es un día de invierno. Yo estoy acostado en la cama debajo de las cubiertas. Un gatito recién nacido está en mi axila izquierda, otro en mi axila derecha, un tercero entre mis piernas y un cuarto en mis manos sobre mi vientre. Yo estoy manteniéndolos calientes. Me siento bien. Me acuerdo, debo haber estado haciendo esto por la noche durante unos días. Una figura de autoridad familiar se entera de esto y saca los gatitos súbitamente sin ninguna consideración mientras me regaña con enojo; entonces... Yo nunca le perdoné por eso, y nunca lo olvidé. Lloré y lloré. Debe haber sido una experiencia realmente traumática para mí. Bien puede ser que por eso desde entonces he estado tratando de compensar a esos gatitos tirados por el inodoro. Sin más preámbulos, aquí dedico esta historia a ellos.

La crueldad a los animales no es algo nuevo. De hecho, la humanidad ha sido cruel con frecuencia. Caramba, la gente ha sido y es a menudo cruel incluso entre sí. ¡Enfrentémoslo! La crueldad es parte de nuestra naturaleza. Dejando la crueldad institucionalizada hacia los animales de lado, creo que hay una conexión entre el estado de vida de la gente y la crueldad hacia los animales. Uno difícilmente puede esperar, por ejemplo, que gente muriendo de hambre en un país desgarrado por la guerra sea amable con los animales, o incluso evite su muerte. La bondad a los animales no es siempre una prioridad. Sin lugar a dudas, las sociedades opulentas ofrecen buenas oportunidades para la vida animal. Voluntarios de toda clase dedican mucho de su tiempo y recursos al cuidado de los animales. Por lo que debe decirse, la bondad hacia los animales, así como la crueldad, debe ser parte de la naturaleza humana. Parece como si el diseño de nuestra naturaleza tiene buenas intenciones, a menos que las circunstancias dicten otra cosa. Sociólogos podrían estar interesados en utilizar esto como una medida para clasificar el estatus del desarrollo de una sociedad. No me extrañaría que en lo más mínimo si ya lo han hecho.

∞∞∞∞

"¿Qué le daremos de comer?" pregunté después de un rato, tomando decisivamente el segundo lugar en materia de crianza, pero al mismo tiempo compensándome por mi toque humano. Verás, "le" como objeto puede referirse "a él" y "a ello" en ruso; y yo, como producto de otro idioma y cultura, estaba pensando claramente en "él", en mi forma subconsciente de personificar al gatito. Esto debe ser un proceso complejo que se produce con los multilingües, cuya hibridación de género puede ser un misterio para los no iniciados.

"No podemos alimentarle nada ahora; no abrirá la boca," dijo Lena. "Lo que necesita es calidez y descanso. Mañana iremos a la ciudad y le conseguiremos un chupete," agregó apagando las luces en la habitación del gatito mientras me empujaba a mí suavemente para que saliera de la habitación.

Salí a nuestro amplio balcón con vistas a la inmensidad oceánica. En algún lugar por ahí, cerca de 8.000 millas en el oeste interminable, estaba Australia, y entremedio una gran cantidad de agua, una fuerza inmensa. En los días de calma, ondas largas acarician pacíficamente la playa como lo han hecho sin descanso y desde tiempo inmemorial. Se me ocurrió que en los días tormentosos, las olas no son tan dóciles. Golpearán la playa sin piedad remodelándola para otro día. Y siempre mantienen la amenaza de tsunami cruel sobre tu cabeza. Sí, algunas veces el mar es bueno, otras veces no lo es. Es también así con la gente y los animales, es la idea.

Estaba maravillando el cielo despejado y su candelabro estrellado flotando sobre el hemisferio sur, pero el frío de la noche que se estaba deslizando rápidamente en mis huesos prescindió abruptamente de mis reflexiones y me obligó a regresar adentro.

∞∞∞∞

Día dos

Nos sentamos a desayunar esperando que nuestro pequeño huésped nos llamara. Ya había echado un vistazo a su caja más de una vez. Traicionando los primeros signos de apego, Lena declaró que debería llevarlo conmigo a mi regreso a América. Ella estaba olvidando que solo habíamos acordado ayudarlo a sobrevivir, y luego devolverlo a su "comunidad" al final de nuestra estadía. No dije nada ya que el proceso de vinculación también había comenzado a enraizarse en mí. La idea de apropiarse del gatito y de una vida juntos ya se me había ocurrido.

Si hubiéramos querido demostrar que somos indiferentes al género, esto podría ser una buena cobertura para la falta de atención o la ignorancia:

"¿Cómo puedes saber si es él o ella?" preguntó Lena. Me sorprendió momentáneamente esta pregunta bastante absurda.

"Si ves dos agujeros, es una ella; de lo contrario, es un él," exclamé con una precisión lacónica mientras lamentaba instantáneamente mi manera grosera. El hecho es que yo tampoco me había dado cuenta; Lo importante era salvar al gatito, no determinar su pertenencia de género, pensé.

Tan pronto como el gatito soltó el primer maullido debil, mi compañera corrió a su lado. La seguí de cerca. Lo recogió con ternura y luego se dirigió a la cocina donde había preparado previamente un gotero con leche de vaca a temperatura ambiente. Este era el tipo de frasco para dejar caer gotas en los ojos, es decir un gotero. Cada vez que el gatito abría la boca para chirriar, ella intentaba echarle un poco de leche. Pero el gatito era demasiado rápido y no estaba dispuesto a dejar pasar la leche. A decir verdad, los dos estábamos algo angustiados, ella más que yo.

"Lo vamos a perder, me temo," se lamentó con una lágrima naciente en su ojo. Después de intentar un par de veces más, se dio por vencida por el momento. Me pidió que sostuviera el gatito mientras rellenaba la botella de agua tibia y remodelaba su cómoda caja con una toalla encima.

Lo que ninguno de nosotros había esperado era el efecto o, mejor dicho -- permítanme ponerlo menos modestamente: la magia de mis manos. Apenas aterrizó en mi palma, dejó de lloriquear; Mis dedos lo acariciaron suavemente detrás de las orejas. De hecho, ahora yo estaba entrando en mi modo de gato experto. Quedó claro que le gustaba mi tratamiento: sus pies se relajaron y su respiración se equilibró. Para subir la apuesta, comencé a tararear y enunciar mis tontos sonidos felinos caseros. Estaba como si ahora estuviéramos en armonía, él y yo.

Lena nos miró a los dos con alivio al determinar que ese era un buen momento para intentar pasar algo de comida. Puso el pulgar y el índice alrededor de su minúscula boca y empujó suavemente la boca para abrirla. Su fila blanca de encías rojizas aparecía a la vista. Lena pudo soltar una gota o dos. Pero el gatito siempre obstinadamente volvía la cabeza. Sin embargo, Lena y yo nos sentíamos que estábamos progresando muy bien. Pasó un minuto y bajó otra gota. Mientras el gatito hacía esto de mala gana, decidimos que era lo suficientemente bueno por el momento. Me lo quitó de la mano y lo puso con cuidado en su caja. Lo cubrió con una toalla dejando solo una grieta para el aire.

"Es una hembra," susurró repentinamente después de que regresáramos a nuestra cena. "Tiene dos agujeros," agregó. La evidencia empírica estaba ahora segura. Sabíamos que teníamos a una hembra.

"Llamémosla Gritis," dijo después de una pausa considerable. "Es gris como tu Gris," continuó. Gris fue mi último gato que fue víctima de mi actividad de trotamundos. Pero esa es otra historia en sí misma.

Así fue como nuestra gatita tenía un género y un nombre y estaba en camino de formar una personalidad en nuestras mentes y corazones.

∞∞∞∞

Día tres

Sin que yo lo supiera, mi compañera se había estado levantando durante la noche para rellenar la botella de agua caliente y tratar de alimentar a Gritis. Se estaba sintiendo frustrada, y la pérdida de sueño la desanimó y angustió más porque sus esfuerzos no dieron ni grandes resultados, ni alentaron una mayor esperanza. Por la mañana me pidió que sostuviera a Gritis de aquella manera "mágica" de siempre, ya que yo me había vuelto al chamán oficial de la casa: Si mis manos no podían hacer el truco, nada podía, fue probablemente la comprensión operativa. Con un par de gotas de leche se nos permitió pasar el estricto control oral de Gritis antes de que volviera a dormir. El agua caliente se rellenó, y una botella de agua caliente adicional se colocó en el exterior adyacente a su caja de zapatos.

Según nuestro plan, aprovechamos de nuestro viaje semanal del sábado a la ciudad no solo para hacer nuestras compras de comestibles sino también para conseguir un chupete para la botella de Gritis. Sin embargo, cuando llegamos a la farmacia, me di cuenta de que no sabía o no podía recordar la palabra en español para chupete. En el impulso del momento decidí usar una táctica antigua: minaría mi mental reserva lingüística y recurriría a una circunlocución. Lo más cercano que pude sacar era la palabra francesa "biberon" para chupete.

"No sé como se dice en español, pero estoy buscando un 'biberon'." Dije usando mi usual manera imperturbable. Para la grata sorpresa de la sensibilidad lingüística de un políglota, el farmacéutico supo de inmediato lo que quería decir y me llevó al mostrador adecuado donde se mostraba una gama completa de todo tipo de chupetes, biberones exquisitos y caros. Había pasado mucho tiempo desde que obtuve algún valor de mi título universario de francés, y alegremente supuse que el farmacéutico debía saber francés hasta que descubrí que existe la misma palabra en español. Las palabras pueden causar muchos problemas y los idiomas constituyen un dolor de cabeza incurable; pero pueden ser muy divertidos e incluso bastante útiles a veces.

∞∞∞∞

No podíamos esperar a volver a casa para probar el nuevo chupete japonés. En su búsqueda en Internet, mi pareja ansiosa, aprendió que la función de succión era importante para la alimentación de los gatitos; ahora íbamos a averiguar si era así. También había leído que, si el gatito no ejerce esta función durante las primeras seis horas de su vida, nunca lo hará. Evidentemente, esta primera succión imparte muchos cultivos microbianos necesarios para poner en marcha la inmunidad de los gatitos. Además, es importante que se cumplan estrictas condiciones higiénicas.

Corrimos a casa con emoción expectante. Gritis ya nos estaba llamando. No quería admitirlo, pero me pareció que sus gritos sonaban un poco más débiles. Aunque no dije nada, la impresión quedó ominosa en mi mente. Gritis se colocó en mi palma, y su pequeña cabeza descansaba entre mi pulgar y mi dedo índice mientras mi señora se dedicaba a preparar una mezcla especial extraída de su búsqueda en Internet. Esto fue considerado como un reemplazo adecuado para la leche de gato. Muy gentilmente, Lena quitó a Gritis de mi mano y trató repetidamente de colocar unas gotas en su boca.

"Lo está tomando," exclamó Lena con alegre gratificación. Una gota entró y luego otra y después de eso otra. Nos miramos con una incredulidad encantadora. Esta cosa funcionó. Estábamos seguros de que este era el punto de inflexión. Alcanzamos hasta felicitarnos y nos sentimos confiados de que la batalla ya estaba ganada. Ahora, Lena estaba pensando en voz alta: nunca se separaría de Gritis. Evidentemente, la unión se estaba sellando.

∞∞∞∞

Día cuatro

Lo primero al levantarnos fue cuidar de Gritis. No puedo explicar por qué, pero quería participar, y lo hacía cada vez que Lena la sacaba de su caja para alimentarla o limpiarla. Había una atracción, un fuerte interés en su bienestar y una alegre anticipación de los buenos tiempos por venir. La gatita se había convertido ahora en nuestro pupilo y estaba a nuestro cuidado. Íbamos a ayudarla a manejar sus muy difíciles primeros pasos en nuestro mundo. De sus búsquedas en Internet, Lena aprendió que, después de alimentarse, masajear suavemente la parte inferior de la barriga de los gatitos provoca la micción. Ella pensó que sería una manera perfecta de comenzar a entrenar a Gritis para ir al baño y ayudar a mantener limpia su área de dormir.

"¿Qué es esto?" preguntó Lena señalando al cordón umbilical seco que todavía colgaba del ombligo de la gatita. Ahora, esta era una pregunta que no se esperaba de una persona sofisticada como mi señora, que resulta ser un médico. Pero también se me ocurrió que yo mismo no había abordado ese tema antes.

"Por supuesto que sabes lo que es; es su cordón umbilical," dije aun preguntándome si Lena simplemente había fallado al preguntar por lo obvio.

"¿Qué haremos con eso?" preguntó mientras colocaba a Gritis en mis manos. Todavía estaba incrédulo de que ella continuaría este juego con seriedad distraída.

"Dame un par de tijeras," dije mirándola desde la esquina del ojo con incredulidad. Era difícil creer que estuviéramos teniendo esta conversación. A decir verdad, Lena no estaba pensando en lo que estaba diciendo; su preocupación por el bienestar de Gritis la había poseído hasta tal punto que sus palabras eran solo palabras sin un significado literal, y no se aplicaban a lo que estaba delante de ella; más bien, eran un escudo para sus temores que consumían su mente. Lena estaba totalmente comprometida con la supervivencia de esta gatita. Saliendo de su ensimismamiento, pronunció:

"Estará bien; crecerá algo más lento y puede que no alcance su peso ideal."

Yo estaba bien con eso. La situación ahora parecía estar bajo control, pero no me estaba olvidando de la importancia de las primeras seis horas de alimentación. Aunque las palabras contrarias querían saltar de mi boca en ese momento, decidí no expresarlas ya que mis dos hembras ahora estaban bien, a pesar del hecho de que no sabíamos si aquella primera alimentación importante había ocurrido en absoluto.

∞∞∞∞

Día cinco

Es de conocimiento general que, en ciertas circunstancias, algunas personas han podido lograr cosas extraordinarias, como una madre que levanta un carro pesado para liberar a su hijo atrapado. Si estas historias son mitos urbanos o un caso de cantidades inusuales de adrenalina no deberían preocuparnos aquí, pero yo estaba tratando de descifrar la transformación que estuvo ante mí. Verás, mi compañera valora tanto su sueño que nada puede interferir con eso. Ella es incansablemente obediente al respecto. Sin embargo, se ha estado levantando más de una vez cada noche para cuidar de Gritis. Lo ha hecho, me explicó, cada vez que la gatita llamaba. Aunque dormimos lado a lado, no escuché nada a pesar del hecho de que se supone que yo duermo más ligeramente. Mi primer pensamiento fue que la diferencia debe estar en el instinto de la madre. Lo que plantea otra pregunta: ¿es el instinto materno transferible? ¿Y puede ser a través de diferentes especies?

Por otro lado, creo que es más sencillo atenerse a explicaciones menos complejas. El alcance comprensivo de Lena puede explicarse por una atracción innata, en algunas personas más fuerte que en otras, por las mascotas. Evidentemente, esto no tiene nada que ver con el instinto materno, ya que tanto el hombre como la mujer quieren mascotas, sino con el factor de la domesticación: la necesidad de esclavizar o ser esclavizados. La humanidad ha domesticado por razones prácticas y no prácticas, formando así lazos y vínculos entre su género y el otro. Quizás esto es lo que estaba operando en este caso. Luego, por alguna razón, recordé unas palabras sabias de Antoine de Saint Exupéry: "Te vuelves responsable para siempre de lo que has domesticado". Esto se sintió como una advertencia donde quizás no se necesitaba ninguna, pero que se cuadraba con mi proclividad para las predicciones lúgubres. Sin embargo, mi pensamiento avanzó: estaba empezando a pensar que la verdadera razón detrás de la afinidad de las personas con las mascotas reside en el simple hecho de que las mascotas satisfacen una necesidad -- la gente necesita confiar, pero teme la traición. De hecho, cuan más desilusionado con la amistad esté uno, y cuan más haya sido traicionado, más probable es que se recurra a las mascotas. Las mascotas parecen venir con una garantía férrea para la amistad incondicional y la de no traición. Para tu mascota, no importa si eres rico o pobre, joven o viejo, hombre o mujer; no importa si tienes sobrepeso o eres delgado, alto o bajo, hermoso o feo. Lo que importa es tú, exclusivamente y categóricamente tú. Tu mascota te otorga un estatus de súper prioridad permanente; tú eres el verdadero Número Uno. Tu mascota nunca te traicionará.

¿Dónde se puede encontrar esta calidad premium de amistad?

Cuando salí de mi confusión mental, la realidad me estaba esperando: Gritis, una vez más, se negaba a comer. Aparte de las escasas comidas, unas pocas gotas de una mezcla recomendada, se mantuvo en curso.

"Creo que se está muriendo," confesó Lena, estallando en lágrimas. Puso sus brazos alrededor de mí, su cabeza apoyada en mi hombro izquierdo mientras sollozaba incontrolablemente por lo que parecía ser un largo rato. Mis esfuerzos por consolarla resultaron ineficaces.

"Lo asesiné," gritó con exageración histriónica mientras se soltaba de nuestro abrazo y retrocedía. Su rostro ahora estaba asumiendo una expresión oscura. Tenía miedo de que ella cayera en uno de sus estados de ánimo de mini depresión.

"¿De qué estás hablando?" me apresuré a arreglar las cosas mientras seguí rápidamente: "Tú has estado haciendo todo lo posible," y continué: "No conozco a nadie que hubiera hecho más." A continuación, procedí a enumerar las muchas cosas que ella había hecho, incluso sacrificar su preciado sueño. Mis esfuerzos parecieron tener solo un menor efecto momentáneo cuando se reanudaron los llantos, aunque algo menos intensos. Parecía que ella estaba decidida a castigarse a sí misma. ¿Qué iba a hacer yo? ¿Debería dejar que esto siga su camino natural y arriesgarme a las consecuencias, o debería continuar con mis aportes útiles?

La batalla del racionalismo contra el emocionalismo estaba en marcha.

∞∞∞∞

Si así era como terminaba la llegada de Gritis a nuestras vidas, entonces ya llegó la hora de que revisara mi pensamiento sobre el significado de las mascotas. Mascotas, que siempre he mantenido, enriquecen nuestras vidas; En gran medida, reflejan y complementan nuestras propias personalidades. ¿Cómo podría un ser tan inocente e inofensivo causar daño? ¿Cómo podrían nuestras mejores intenciones y acciones ejemplares conducir a un dolor involuntario?

∞∞∞∞

Dia seis

Tengo que ser franco: las cosas no van muy bien. Lena se ha vuelto más tranquila de lo habitual. Mientras me he puesto en el llamado perpetuo para las sesiones de curación manual, Lena a diario continúa limpiando a Gritis y no pierde la oportunidad de intentar alimentarla. Nunca pierde una de sus llamadas de día o de noche. Este es un lado de ella que yo no había visto antes. Estaba revisando mi evaluación de sus rasgos egoístas. Estaba claramente abatida y bastante descorazonada ya que la gatita ahora ha cerrado la boca. Yo estaba preocupado por lo que iba a venir a continuación. La situación también me estaba afectando, y estaba empezando a andar de puntillas alrededor de ella y de toda esta situación. Ahora estábamos envueltos por un humor sombrío. Ambos sabíamos que estábamos perdiendo terreno, pero yo todavía no quería rendirme. El pensamiento acerca de la primera alimentación crítica pasó por mi mente inquieta una vez más. Y decidí hacer algo al respecto por mi cuenta. Sin ningún plan específico en mente, bajé las escaleras y marché agresivamente hacia la portería, donde dos asistentes charlaban.

"¿Quién de ustedes ha estado tirando a los gatitos?" me oí interrogando. Como si hubiera sido ensayado, sus bocas se abrieron mientras me miraban con incredulidad, y luego se miraron rápidamente, aparentemente preguntándose si no había perdido un tornillo. Me aseguraron que nadie arroja a los gatitos, pero sí que algunos gatos lo hacen. Y uno de ellos, refiriéndose a la madre de Gritis, continuó:

"De hecho, este gato en particular abandonó a otro de sus recién nacidos allí," y señaló dónde estaban algunos arbustos grandes. Antes de que pudiera correr allí en seguida, me detuvo explicando que no había nada allí ahora. No tuve el corazón para preguntar qué le había pasado a la hermana de Gritis. Pensé que me lo habrían dicho si fueran buenas noticias.

A veces, es mejor no saber.

∞∞∞∞

Dia siete

Cuando sale el sol, nos gusta desayunar en el lado este; se siente bien dejar que el suave sol de la mañana nos haga pasar al nuevo día. Acababa de empezar a desayunar cuando Lena entró silenciosamente en la habitación y me entregó a Gritis.

"Держи! (¡tenla!)," dijo sin ánimo. Como solía hacer, pensó que algo de "energía vital" de mis manos haría que Gritis se sintiera mejor.

Sostuve a la gatita durante mucho tiempo mientras tarareaba una dulce pero triste melodía griega sobre un ser querido que los trenes habían alejado. La elección de la canción fue totalmente fortuita: a primera hora de la mañana, había captado su primer par de compases mientras revisaba los archivos en mi mp3. Continué sosteniendo a Gritis, con su cara alejada del sol, para que el sol débil de la mañana calentara la pequeña parte que mis manos no podían cubrir. Esto pareció relajarla un poco y consolarme un poco a mí, pero nuestra pequeña amiga, todavía negándose a comer, aún con los ojos cerrados, ahora estaba recostada. Y seguí esperezándome a la idea de que ella solo estaba descansando y que iba a estar bien.

¡Oh, cuán cegadora puede ser la esperanza!

Escuché el llanto prolongado y silencioso de Lena en la habitación contigua. Ella lo sabía mejor, y ahora evidentemente se había dado por vencida. Sintiéndose como un completo fracaso, regresó a la sala de desayunos, donde estábamos Gritis y yo, con los ojos llenos de lágrimas. Tenía algo que decirme, se las arregló para murmurar. Frunció los ojos, fijó su mirada en la mía y dejó escapar: la novia de su hermano, que trabajó un rato en una clínica de abortos, le había dicho que solían a colocar a los fetos abortados cerca de un calentador para aliviar su muerte. Ella sabía que la gatita se estaba muriendo en ese día, y explicó por qué quería que mis manos fueran lo que el calentador podría haber sido para los fetos abortados vivos.

La asociación y el momento me parecieron extraños. Intuí que todo este episodio de principio al fin no fue accidental; que casi nada nos llega por casualidad, pero siempre con un mensaje que se desperdicia solo si no estamos preparados, o no podemos recibirlo, para resolverlo. Un torrente de pensamientos corrió por mi cabeza. Las comparaciones involuntarias bombardearon mi cerebro amenazando algunas nociones muy arraigadas sobre la vida. Luché por concentrarme en la tarea en cuestión, para no dejar que mi mente se alejara ahora. Partecitas de mi lenguaje felino se reanudaron momentáneamente, antes de que el mensaje se apoderara por completo. Mis ojos se clavaron en la gatita. Me pregunté si el flujo de energía realmente se había invertido, ya no de mí a Gritis, sino al revés. Y en una fracción de segundo, todo quedó claro, o al menos eso pensé: se envió un mensaje; se había abierto paso hasta mí y lo había recibido: *la vida es más preciosa de lo que se cree.*

Masajeé suavemente las minúsculas piernas de Gritis; estaban inmóviles. Movió su pequeña cabeza muy ligeramente como para indicar que estaba contenta, complacida y satisfecha: su misión ya estaba cumplida. Vi signos sólidos como estaba dejando escapar un suspiro más grande; Las diminutas piernas se movían ligeramente una vez más.

Y entonces, de repente, ya no estaba más.

∞∞∞∞

Un poco más tarde, hice esta entrada en mi diario: "La gatita murió hace una hora después de que pude sostenerla en mis manos durante unos 30 minutos, tiempo durante el cual la ví relajarse y exhalar por última vez. Los siete días de pasión de Gritis llegaron a su fin hoy. Lena lloró mucho y todavía está de luto. Quería que nosotros sepultáramos a Gritis donde solíamos pasar las mañanas, en el oratorio al lado del área de recreación; le sugerí que eligiera un lugar diferente para evitar un triste recordatorio diario. Al fin accedió a enterrarla en la playa, lo cual hice yo.

Fue una experiencia emocional para mí, pero lo hice con gran reverencia y de una manera que corresponde a un ser vivo. No pude contener mis lágrimas. No hay duda de que soy sentimental. Siempre he sido así. Por encima de todo, me emocioné por razones personales: ¿crees que inundamos con amor a nuestras mascotas porque no ha sido así con nosotros mismos? Lena también demostró ser un alma de buen corazón. Pude ver otro lado bueno de ella. La llegada de Gritis a nuestras vidas estaba cargada de significado y sentido. Su breve presencia nos ayudó a descubrir y comprender cosas sobre nosotros mismos que ignorábamos o habíamos olvidado. Había muchas razones para estar realmente agradecido con ella, con una gatita de corta duración llamada Gritis."

∞∞∞∞

Día once

Me dispuse a ir al bosque donde Lena me estaba esperando. Decidí ir por la playa. Mientras pasaba por donde había enterrado a Gritis hacía solo cuatro días, busqué el palo que marcaba su tumba. Como no había nada que ver, me acerqué. El túmulo de arena que había formado había sido demolido, y un agujero había ocupado su lugar; los pedazos masticados de la bolsa azul donde había colocado a Gritis podían verse dispersos. Evidentemente, su carne en descomposición había emitido suficiente olor a través de la bolsa y de la pila de arena para atraer a algunos animales carnívoros, probablemente uno de esos hambrientos perros errantes.

Y así, nada quedó de Gritis y nada se desperdició: significativa en la vida y beneficiosa en la muerte.

Papudo, Chile,
Marzo 2012

(Traducido del inglés por el autor.)

THE END

* 9 7 9 8 2 1 8 2 8 6 6 2 0 *